MznLnx

Missing Links Exam Preps

Exam Prep for

Numerical Methods

Faires & Burden, 3rd Edition

The MznLnx Exam Prep is your link from the texbook and lecture to your exams.
The MznLnx Exam Preps are unauthorized and comprehensive reviews of your textbooks.

All material provided by MznLnx and Rico Publications (c) 2010
Textbook publishers and textbook authors do not particpate in or contribute to these reviews.

MznLnx

Rico Publications

Exam Prep for Numerical Methods
3rd Edition
Faires & Burden

Publisher: Raymond Houge
Assistant Editor: Michael Rouger
Text and Cover Designer: Lisa Buckner
Marketing Manager: Sara Swagger
Project Manager, Editorial Production: Jerry Emerson
Art Director: Vernon Lowerui

Product Manager: Dave Mason
Editorial Assitant: Rachel Guzmanji
Pedagogy: Debra Long
Cover Image: Jim Reed/Getty Images
Text and Cover Printer: City Printing, Inc.
Compositor: Media Mix, Inc.

(c) 2010 Rico Publications

ALL RIGHTS RESERVED. No part of this work covered by the copyright may be reproduced or used in any form or by an means--graphic, electronic, or mechanical, including photocopying, recording, taping, Web distribution, information storage, and retrieval systems, or in any other manner--without the written permission of the publisher.

Printed in the United States
ISBN:

For more information about our products, contact us at:
Dave.Mason@RicoPublications.com

For permission to use material from this text or product, submit a request online to:
Dave.Mason@RicoPublications.com

Contents

CHAPTER 1
Mathematical Preliminaries and Error Analysis — 1

CHAPTER 2
Solutions of Equations of One Variable — 11

CHAPTER 3
Interpolation and Polynomial Approximation — 18

CHAPTER 4
Numerical Integration and Differentiation — 26

CHAPTER 5
Numerical Solution of Initial-Value Problems — 36

CHAPTER 6
Direct Methods for Solving Linear Systems — 45

CHAPTER 7
Iterative Methods for Solving Linear Systems — 62

CHAPTER 8
Approximation Theory — 73

CHAPTER 9
Approximating Eigenvalues — 83

CHAPTER 10
Solutions of Systems of Nonlinear Equations — 92

CHAPTER 11
Boundary-Value Problems for Ordinary Differential Equations — 97

CHAPTER 12
Numerical Methods for Partial-Differential Equations — 102

ANSWER KEY — 109

TO THE STUDENT

COMPREHENSIVE

The *MznLnx* Exam Prep series is designed to help you pass your exams. Editors at *MznLnx* review your textbooks and then prepare these practice exams to help you master the textbook material. Unlike study guides, workbooks, and practice tests provided by the texbook publisher and textbook authors, *MznLnx* gives you **all** of the material in each chapter in exam form, not just samples, so you can be sure to nail your exam.

MECHANICAL

The MznLnx Exam Prep series creates exams that will help you learn the subject matter as well as test you on your understanding. Each question is designed to help you master the concept. Just working through the exams, you gain an understanding of the subject--its a simple mechanical process that produces success.

INTEGRATED STUDY GUIDE AND REVIEW

MznLnx is not just a set of exams designed to test you, its also a comprehensive review of the subject content. Each exam question is also a review of the concept, making sure that you will get the answer correct without having to go to other sources of material. You learn as you go! Its the easiest way to pass an exam.

HUMOR

Studying can be tedious and dry. MznLnx's instructional design includes moderate humor within the exam questions on occassion, to break the tedium and revitalize the brain

Chapter 1. Mathematical Preliminaries and Error Analysis

1. _____ is a term in mathematics. It can refer to:

   - a _____ line, in geometry
   - the trigonometric function called _____
   - the _____ method, a root-finding algorithm in numerical analysis

   a. Large set
   b. Solvable
   c. Separable
   d. Secant

2. In probability theory, a probability distribution is called _____ if its cumulative distribution function is _____. That is equivalent to saying that for random variables X with the distribution in question, Pr[X = a] = 0 for all real numbers a. If the distribution of X is _____ then X is called a _____ random variable.
   a. Continuous phase modulation
   b. Concatenated codes
   c. Conull set
   d. Continuous

3. In mathematics, a _____ is a function for which, intuitively, small changes in the input result in small changes in the output. Otherwise, a function is said to be discontinuous. A _____ with a continuous inverse function is called bicontinuous.
   a. Beth numbers
   b. Continuous function
   c. Contraction mapping
   d. Charles's Law

4. The mathematical concept of a _____ expresses the intuitive idea of deterministic dependence between two quantities, one of which is viewed as primary and the other as secondary. A _____ then is a way to associate a unique output for each input of a specified type, for example, a real number or an element of a given set.
   a. Coherent
   b. Grill
   c. Going up
   d. Function

5. In mathematics, the concept of a '_____' is used to describe the behavior of a function as its argument or input either 'gets close' to some point, or as the argument becomes arbitrarily large; or the behavior of a sequence's elements as their index increases indefinitely. _____s are used in calculus and other branches of mathematical analysis to define derivatives and continuity.

   In formulas, _____ is usually abbreviated as lim.

   a. Copula
   b. Contact
   c. Duality
   d. Limit

6. As the positive integer n becomes larger and larger, the value n si becomes arbitrarily close to 1. We say that 'the limit of the sequence n si equals 1.'

   The _____ is one of the oldest concepts in mathematical analysis. It provides a rigorous definition of the idea of a sequence converging towards a point called the limit.

   a. Moment problem
   b. Darboux function
   c. Differential calculus
   d. Limit of a sequence

Chapter 1. Mathematical Preliminaries and Error Analysis

7. In mathematics, an _____ in the sense of ring theory is a subring $\mathcal{O}$ of a ring R that satisfies the conditions

   1. R is a ring which is a finite-dimensional algebra over the rational number field $\mathbb{Q}$
   2. $\mathcal{O}$ spans R over $\mathbb{Q}$, so that $\mathbb{Q}\mathcal{O} = R$, and
   3. $\mathcal{O}$ is a lattice in R.

The third condition can be stated more accurately, in terms of the extension of scalars of R to the real numbers, embedding R in a real vector space. In less formal terms, additively $\mathcal{O}$ should be a free abelian group generated by a basis for R over $\mathbb{Q}$.

The leading example is the case where R is a number field K and $\mathcal{O}$ is its ring of integers. In algebraic number theory there are examples for any K other than the rational field of proper subrings of the ring of integers that are also _____s.

   a. Order
   c. Annihilator
   b. Efficiency
   d. Algebraic

8. The _____ Evaluation and Review Technique, commonly abbreviated PERT, is a model for project management designed to analyze and represent the tasks involved in completing a given project.

PERT is a method to analyze the involved tasks in completing a given project, especially the time needed to complete each task, and identifying the minimum time needed to complete the total project.

This model was invented by Booz Allen Hamilton, Inc.

   a. Battle of the Sexes
   c. Key server
   b. Huge
   d. Program

9. The multiple integral is a type of definite integral extended to functions of more than one real variable, for example, fz = x^2 + y^2. The rectangular region at the bottom of the body is the domain of integration, while the surface is the graph of the two-variable function to be integrated.

Introduction

Just as the definite integral of a positive function of one variable represents the area of the region between the graph of the function and the x-axis, the _____ of a positive function of two variables represents the volume of the region between the surface defined by the function and the plane which contains its domain.

Chapter 1. Mathematical Preliminaries and Error Analysis

a. Signed measure
b. Solid of revolution
c. Risch algorithm
d. Double Integral

10. In commutative algebra, the notions of an element _____ over a ring, and of an _____ extension of rings, are a generalization of the notions in field theory of an element being algebraic over a field, and of an algebraic extension of fields.

The special case of greatest interest in number theory is that of complex numbers _____ over the ring of integers Z.

The term ring will be understood to mean commutative ring with a unit.

a. Arc length
b. Integral
c. Integral test for convergence
d. Antidifferentiation

11. In applied mathematics and mechanical engineering, the _____ is a widely used, classical method for the calculation of the natural vibration frequency of a structure in the second or higher order. It is a direct variational method in which the minimum of a functional defined on a normed linear space is approximated by a linear combination of elements from that space. This method will yield solutions when an analytical form for the true solution may be intractable.

a. 1-center problem
b. 2-3 heap
c. 120-cell
d. Rayleigh-Ritz method

12. _____ of the difference quotient as h approaches zero, if this limit exists. If the limit exists, then f is _____ at a. Here f' (a) is one of several common notations for the derivative

a. 2-3 heap
b. 120-cell
c. Differentiable
d. 1-center problem

13. In calculus, the _____ states that if a real-valued function f is continuous in the closed interval, then f must attain its maximum and minimum value, each at least once.

a. Average cost
b. Uncertainty quantification
c. Equity
d. Extreme Value Theorem

14. In statistics, _____ has two related meanings:

- the arithmetic _____.
- the expected value of a random variable, which is also called the population _____.

It is sometimes stated that the '_____' _____s average. This is incorrect if '_____' is taken in the specific sense of 'arithmetic _____' as there are different types of averages: the _____, median, and mode. For instance, average house prices almost always use the median value for the average.

For a real-valued random variable X, the _____ is the expectation of X.

a. Mean
b. Statistical population
c. Probability
d. Proportional hazards model

Chapter 1. Mathematical Preliminaries and Error Analysis

15. In calculus, the _____ states, roughly, that given a section of a smooth curve, there is at least one point on that section at which the derivative of the curve is equal to the 'average' derivative of the section. It is used to prove theorems that make global conclusions about a function on an interval starting from local hypotheses about derivatives at points of the interval.

This theorem can be understood concretely by applying it to motion: if a car travels one hundred miles in one hour, so that its average speed during that time was 100 miles per hour, then at some time its instantaneous speed must have been exactly 100 miles per hour.

a. Fundamental Theorem of Calculus
b. Calculus controversy
c. Functional integration
d. Mean Value Theorem

16. In mathematics, a _____ is a statement that can be proved on the basis of explicitly stated or previously agreed assumptions.

a. Disjunction introduction
b. Theorem
c. Boolean function
d. Logical value

17. A _____ is is a graphical technique for presenting a data set drawn by hand or produced by a mechanical or electronic plotter. It is a graph depicting the relationship between two or more variables used, for instance, in visualising scientific data.

_____s play an important role in statistics and data analysis.

a. C-35
b. Dini
c. Lattice
d. Plot

18. Georg Friedrich Bernhard _____ was a German mathematician who made important contributions to analysis and differential geometry, some of them paving the way for the later development of general relativity.

_____ was born in Breselenz, a village near Dannenberg in the Kingdom of Hanover in what is today Germany. His father, Friedrich Bernhard _____, was a poor Lutheran pastor in Breselenz who fought in the Napoleonic Wars.

a. Gustave Bertrand
b. Paul C. van Oorschot
c. Brook Taylor
d. Riemann

19. In the branch of mathematics known as real analysis, the _____, created by Bernhard Riemann, was the first rigorous definition of the integral of a function on an interval. While the _____ is unsuitable for many theoretical purposes, it is one of the easiest integrals to define. Some of these technical deficiencies can be remedied by the Riemann-Stieltjes integral, and most of them disappear in the Lebesgue integral.

a. Riemann integral
b. Skorokhod integral
c. Darboux integral
d. Russo-Vallois integral

20. In mathematics and in the sciences, a _____ (plural: _____e, formulæ or _____s) is a concise way of expressing information symbolically (as in a mathematical or chemical _____), or a general relationship between quantities. One of many famous _____e is Albert Einstein's $E = mc^2$ (see special relativity

In mathematics, a _____ is a key to solve an equation with variables. For example, the problem of determining the volume of a sphere is one that requires a significant amount of integral calculus to solve.

a. 2-3 heap
c. 120-cell

b. 1-center problem
d. Formula

21. The _____ in some data is the discrepancy between an exact value and some approximation to it. An _____ can occur because

1. the measurement of the data is not precise, or
2. approximations are used instead of the real data.

In the mathematical field of numerical analysis, the numerical stability of an algorithm in numerical analysis indicates how the error is propagated by the algorithm.

One commonly distinguishes between the relative error and the absolute error. The absolute error is the magnitude of the difference between the exact value and the approximation.

a. A posteriori
c. A Mathematical Theory of Communication

b. Approximation error
d. A chemical equation

22. Augustin-Jean _____ (10 May 1788 - 14 July 1827), was a French physicist who contributed significantly to the establishment of the theory of wave optics. _____ studied the behaviour of light both theoretically and experimentally.

_____ was the son of an architect, born at Broglie (Eure.)

a. Ralph C. Merkle
c. Kaisa Nyberg

b. James Dickson Murray
d. Fresnel

23. _____, S(x) and C(x), are two transcendental functions named after Augustin-Jean Fresnel that are used in optics. They arise in the description of near field Fresnel diffraction phenomena, and are defined through the following integral representations:

$$S(x) = \int_0^x \sin(t^2)\, dt, \quad C(x) = \int_0^x \cos(t^2)\, dt.$$

The simultaneous parametric plot of S(x) and C(x) is the Cornu spiral, or clothoid.

Normalised _____, S(x) and C(x).
a. Logarithmic spiral
c. Spiral

b. Spiral of Theodorus
d. Fresnel integrals

24. In mathematics, an _____, or central tendency of a data set refers to a measure of the 'middle' or 'expected' value of the data set. There are many different descriptive statistics that can be chosen as a measurement of the central tendency of the data items.

An _____ is a single value that is meant to typify a list of values.

a. Average
b. A posteriori
c. A Mathematical Theory of Communication
d. A chemical equation

25. In mathematical analysis, the _____ states that for each value between the least upper bound and greatest lower bound of the image of a continuous function there is a corresponding value in its domain mapping to the original. _____

- Version I. The _____ states the following: If the function y = f∈ [a, b] such that f

- Version II. Suppose that I is an interval [a, b] in the real numbers R and that f : I → R is a continuous function. Then the image set f

    f⊇ [f or f(I) ⊇ [f(b), f(a)].

It is frequently stated in the following equivalent form: Suppose that f : [a, b] → R is continuous and that u is a real number satisfying f(a) < u < f(b) or f(a) > u > f(b.) Then for some c ∈ [a, b], f(c) = u.

This captures an intuitive property of continuous functions: given f continuous on [1, 2], if f(1) = 3 and f(2) = 5 then f must take the value 4 somewhere between 1 and 2.

a. Equicontinuous
b. A Mathematical Theory of Communication
c. Uniformly continuous
d. Intermediate Value Theorem

26. In mathematics, a _____ is an expression constructed from variables and constants, using the operations of addition, subtraction, multiplication, and constant non-negative whole number exponents. For example, $x^2 - 4x + 7$ is a _____, but $x^2 - 4/x + 7x^{3/2}$ is not, because its second term involves division by the variable x and also because its third term contains an exponent that is not a whole number.

_____s are one of the most important concepts in algebra and throughout mathematics and science.

a. Coimage
b. Group extension
c. Semifield
d. Polynomial

27. In mathematics, a _____ is often represented as the sum of a sequence of terms. That is, a _____ is represented as a list of numbers with addition operations between them, for example this arithmetic sequence:

   1 + 2 + 3 + 4 + 5 + ... + 99 + 100

In most cases of interest the terms of the sequence are produced according to a certain rule, such as by a formula, by an algorithm, by a sequence of measurements, or even by a random number generator.

a. Blind
b. Series
c. Contact
d. Concavity

28. In statistics, _____ results in values that are limited above or below, similar to but distinct from the concept of statistical censoring.

Usually the values that insurance adjusters receive are either left-truncated, right-censored or both. For example, if policyholders are subject to a policy limit u, then any loss amounts that are actually above u are reported to the insurance company as being exactly u because u is the amount the insurance companies pay.

a. Numerical analysis
b. Fixed point iteration
c. Truncation
d. Descriptive research

29. _____ or local _____ is error made by numerical algorithms that arises from taking finite number of steps in computation. It is present even with infinite-precision arithmetic, because it is caused by truncation of the infinite Taylor series to form the algorithm.

Use of arbitrarily small steps in numerical computation is prevented by round-off error, which are the consequence of using finite precision floating point numbers on computers.

a. Biarc
b. Truncation error
c. Low-discrepancy sequence
d. Numerical analysis

30. In mathematics, the _____ is a term used to describe the number of times one must apply a given operation to an integer before reaching a fixed point.

Usually, this refers to the additive or multiplicative persistence of an integer, which is how often one has to replace the number by the sum or product of its digits until one reaches a single digit. Because the numbers are broken down into their digits, the additive or multiplicative persistence depends on the radix.

a. Persistence of a number
b. Linear congruence theorem
c. Coprime
d. Lychrel number

31. In linear algebra, functional analysis and related areas of mathematics, a _____ is a function that assigns a strictly positive length or size to all vectors in a vector space, other than the zero vector. A seminorm, on the other hand, is allowed to assign zero length to some non-zero vectors.

A simple example is the 2-dimensional Euclidean space R^2 equipped with the Euclidean _____.

a. Compression
b. Going up
c. Leibniz formula
d. Norm

32. The Institute of Electrical and Electronics Engineers or _____ (read eye-triple-e) is an international non-profit, professional organization for the advancement of technology related to electricity. It has the most members of any technical professional organization in the world, with more than 365,000 members in around 150 countries.

The _____ is incorporated in the State of New York, United States.

a. A chemical equation
b. A Mathematical Theory of Communication
c. A posteriori
d. IEEE

33. In linear algebra, _____ is an efficient algorithm for solving systems of linear equations, finding the rank of a matrix, and calculating the inverse of an invertible square matrix. _____ is named after German mathematician and scientist Carl Friedrich Gauss.

Elementary row operations are used to reduce a matrix to row echelon form.

a. Crout matrix decomposition
b. Gaussian elimination
c. Conjugate gradient method
d. Cholesky decomposition

34. In mathematics, two vectors are _____ if they are perpendicular. For example, a subway and the street above, although they do not physically intersect, are _____ if they cross at a right angle.
a. Algebraic structure
b. Orthogonal
c. Additive identity
d. Unique factorization domain

35. A _____ is the difference between the calculated approximation of a number and its exact mathematical value. Numerical analysis specifically tries to estimate this error when using approximation equations and/or algorithms, especially when using finite digits to represent infinite digits of real numbers. This is a form of quantization error.
a. Round-off error
b. Large eddy simulation
c. Numerical model of the solar system
d. Minimum polynomial extrapolation

36. _____ involves reducing the number of significant digits in a number. The result of _____ is a 'shorter' number having fewer non-zero digits yet similar in magnitude. The result is less precise but easier to use.
a. Sudan function
b. Shabakh
c. Hyper operator
d. Rounding

37. In mathematics, particularly linear algebra and numerical analysis, the _____ is a method for orthogonalizing a set of vectors in an inner product space, most commonly the Euclidean space R^n. The _____ takes a finite, linearly independent set S = {v_1, ââ,¬¦, v_n} and generates an orthogonal set S' = {u_1, ââ,¬¦, u_n} that spans the same subspace as S.

The method is named for J>ørgen Pedersen Gram and Erhard Schmidt but it appeared earlier in the work of Laplace and Cauchy.

a. Dot product
b. Gram-Schmidt process
c. Linear algebra
d. Homogeneous coordinates

38. In model theory, a complete theory is called _____ if it does not have too many types. One goal of classification theory is to divide all complete theories into those whose models can be classified and those whose models are too complicated to classify, and to classify all models in the cases where this can be done. Roughly speaking, if a theory is not _____ then its models are too complicated and numerous to classify, while if a theory is _____ there might be some hope of classifying its models, especially if the theory is superstable or totally transcendental.

a. Transfer principle
b. Non-standard calculus
c. Stable
d. Spectrum of a theory

39. _____ occurs when the growth rate of a mathematical function is proportional to the function's current value. In the case of a discrete domain of definition with equal intervals it is also called geometric growth or geometric decay.

With _____ of a positive value its rate of increase steadily increases, or in the case of exponential decay, its rate of decrease steadily decreases.

a. A chemical equation
b. Exponential growth
c. A posteriori
d. A Mathematical Theory of Communication

40. A _____ is a simple shape of Euclidean geometry consisting of those points in a plane which are at a constant distance, called the radius, from a fixed point, called the center. A _____ with center A is sometimes denoted by the symbol A.

A chord of a _____ is a line segment whose two endpoints lie on the _____.

a. Circumcircle
b. Malfatti circles
c. Circular segment
d. Circle

41. Leonardo of Pisa (c. 1170 - c. 1250), also known as Leonardo Pisano, Leonardo Bonacci, Leonardo _____, or, most commonly, simply _____, was an Italian mathematician, considered by some 'the most talented mathematician of the Middle Ages'.
a. Ralph C. Merkle
b. Guido Castelnuovo
c. Harry Hinsley
d. Fibonacci

42. In mathematics and the arts, two quantities are in the _____ if the ratio between the sum of those quantities and the larger one is the same as the ratio between the larger one and the smaller. The _____ is an irrational mathematical constant, approximately 1.6180339887.

At least since the Renaissance, many artists and architects have proportioned their works to approximate the _____ -- especially in the form of the golden rectangle, in which the ratio of the longer side to the shorter is the _____ --believing this proportion to be aesthetically pleasing.

a. 120-cell
b. 1-center problem
c. Golden ratio
d. 2-3 heap

43. In mathematics, an _____ or member of a set is any one of the distinct objects that make up that set.

Writing A = {1,2,3,4}, means that the _____s of the set A are the numbers 1, 2, 3 and 4. Groups of _____s of A, for example {1,2}, are subsets of A.

a. Universal code
b. Ideal
c. Order
d. Element

44. In mathematics, computing, linguistics and related subjects, an _____ is a sequence of finite instructions, often used for calculation and data processing. It is formally a type of effective method in which a list of well-defined instructions for completing a task will, when given an initial state, proceed through a well-defined series of successive states, eventually terminating in an end-state. The transition from one state to the next is not necessarily deterministic; some _____s, known as probabilistic _____s, incorporate randomness.

   a. In-place algorithm   b. Out-of-core
   c. Approximate counting algorithm   d. Algorithm

45. In acoustics and telecommunication, the _____ of a wave is a component frequency of the signal that is an integer multiple of the fundamental frequency. For example, if the frequency is f, the _____s have frequency 2f, 3f, 4f, etc, as well as f itself. The _____s have the property that they are all periodic at the signal frequency.

   a. Subharmonic   b. Digital room correction
   c. Robinson-Dadson curves   d. Harmonic

46. In mathematics, the _____ is the infinite series

$$\sum_{k=1}^{\infty} \frac{1}{k} = 1 + \frac{1}{2} + \frac{1}{3} + \frac{1}{4} + \cdots .$$

Its name derives from the concept of overtones, or harmonics, in music: the wavelengths of the overtones of a vibrating string are 1/2, 1/3, 1/4, etc., of the string's fundamental wavelength. Every term of the series after the first is the harmonic mean of the neighboring terms; the term harmonic mean likewise derives from music.

The _____ diverges to infinity, albeit rather slowly.

   a. Character   b. Concavity
   c. Bandwidth   d. Harmonic series

Chapter 2. Solutions of Equations of One Variable

1. The _____ , is achieved in a packed stadium when successive groups of spectators briefly stand and raise their arms. Each spectator is required to rise at the same time as those straight in front and behind, and slightly after the person immediately to either the right or the left. Immediately upon stretching to full height, the spectator returns to the usual seated position.
   - a. Wave
   - b. Thermodynamic limit
   - c. Lagrangian
   - d. Pauli exclusion principle

2. The _____ is an important second-order linear partial differential equation that describes the propagation of a variety of waves, such as sound waves, light waves and water waves. It arises in fields such as acoustics, electromagnetics, and fluid dynamics. Historically, the problem of a vibrating string such as that of a musical instrument was studied by Jean le Rond d'Alembert, Leonhard Euler, Daniel Bernoulli, and Joseph-Louis Lagrange.
   - a. Random walk
   - b. Wave Equation
   - c. Lagrangian
   - d. Cauchy momentum equation

3. In mathematics, the _____ is a root-finding algorithm which repeatedly divides an interval in half and then selects the subinterval in which a root exists. It is a very simple and robust method, but it is also rather slow.

   Suppose we want to solve the equation

   $$f(x) = 0,$$

   where f is a continuous function.

   - a. 1-center problem
   - b. 120-cell
   - c. Secant method
   - d. Bisection method

4. The _____ Evaluation and Review Technique, commonly abbreviated PERT, is a model for project management designed to analyze and represent the tasks involved in completing a given project.

   PERT is a method to analyze the involved tasks in completing a given project, especially the time needed to complete each task, and identifying the minimum time needed to complete the total project.

   This model was invented by Booz Allen Hamilton, Inc.

   - a. Key server
   - b. Program
   - c. Battle of the Sexes
   - d. Huge

5. In vascular plants, the _____ is the organ of a plant body that typically lies below the surface of the soil. This is not always the case, however, since a _____ can also be aerial (that is, growing above the ground) or aerating (that is, growing up above the ground or especially above water.) Furthermore, a stem normally occurring below ground is not exceptional either
   - a. Root
   - b. 120-cell
   - c. 2-3 heap
   - d. 1-center problem

6. The mathematical concept of a _____ expresses the intuitive idea of deterministic dependence between two quantities, one of which is viewed as primary and the other as secondary. A _____ then is a way to associate a unique output for each input of a specified type, for example, a real number or an element of a given set.

Chapter 2. Solutions of Equations of One Variable

    a. Going up
    c. Coherent
    b. Grill
    d. Function

7. In mathematics and in the sciences, a _____ (plural: _____e, formulæ or _____s) is a concise way of expressing information symbolically (as in a mathematical or chemical _____), or a general relationship between quantities. One of many famous _____e is Albert Einstein's E = mc² (see special relativity

In mathematics, a _____ is a key to solve an equation with variables. For example, the problem of determining the volume of a sphere is one that requires a significant amount of integral calculus to solve.

    a. 2-3 heap
    c. 120-cell
    b. 1-center problem
    d. Formula

8. In mathematics, a _____ is a statement that can be proved on the basis of explicitly stated or previously agreed assumptions.
    a. Logical value
    c. Boolean function
    b. Disjunction introduction
    d. Theorem

9. _____ is a term in mathematics. It can refer to:

- a _____ line, in geometry
- the trigonometric function called _____
- the _____ method, a root-finding algorithm in numerical analysis

    a. Solvable
    c. Secant
    b. Separable
    d. Large set

10. In numerical analysis, the _____ is a root-finding algorithm that uses a succession of roots of secant lines to better approximate a root of a function f. The first two iterations of the _____. The red curve shows the function f and the blue lines are the secants.

The _____ is defined by the recurrence relation

$$x_{n+1} = x_n - \frac{x_n - x_{n-1}}{f(x_n) - f(x_{n-1})} f(x_n).$$

As can be seen from the recurrence relation, the _____ requires two initial values, x_0 and x_1, which should ideally be chosen to lie close to the root.

    a. Convolutional code
    c. Biconnected
    b. Secant method
    d. Bar product

11. In commutative algebra, the notions of an element _____ over a ring, and of an _____ extension of rings, are a generalization of the notions in field theory of an element being algebraic over a field, and of an algebraic extension of fields.

Chapter 2. Solutions of Equations of One Variable 13

The special case of greatest interest in number theory is that of complex numbers _____ over the ring of integers Z.

The term ring will be understood to mean commutative ring with a unit.

- a. Antidifferentiation
- b. Arc length
- c. Integral
- d. Integral test for convergence

12. In statistics, _____ has two related meanings:

- the arithmetic _____.
- the expected value of a random variable, which is also called the population _____.

It is sometimes stated that the '_____' _____s average. This is incorrect if '_____' is taken in the specific sense of 'arithmetic _____' as there are different types of averages: the _____, median, and mode. For instance, average house prices almost always use the median value for the average.

For a real-valued random variable X, the _____ is the expectation of X.

- a. Mean
- b. Statistical population
- c. Probability
- d. Proportional hazards model

13. In calculus, the _____ states, roughly, that given a section of a smooth curve, there is at least one point on that section at which the derivative of the curve is equal to the 'average' derivative of the section. It is used to prove theorems that make global conclusions about a function on an interval starting from local hypotheses about derivatives at points of the interval.

This theorem can be understood concretely by applying it to motion: if a car travels one hundred miles in one hour, so that its average speed during that time was 100 miles per hour, then at some time its instantaneous speed must have been exactly 100 miles per hour.

- a. Mean Value Theorem
- b. Functional integration
- c. Fundamental Theorem of Calculus
- d. Calculus controversy

14. The _____ (symbol: N) is the SI derived unit of force, named after Isaac _____ in recognition of his work on classical mechanics.

The _____ is the unit of force derived in the SI system; it is equal to the amount of force required to accelerate a mass of one kilogram at a rate of one meter per second per second. Algebraically:

$$1 \text{ N} = 1 \ \frac{\text{kg} \cdot \text{m}}{\text{s}^2}.$$

- 1 N is the force of Earth's gravity on an object with a mass of about 102 g ($\frac{1}{9.8}$ kg) (such as a small apple.)
- On Earth's surface, a mass of 1 kg exerts a force of approximately 9.80665 N [down] (or 1 kgf.) The approximation of 1 kg corresponding to 10 N is sometimes used as a rule of thumb in everyday life and in engineering.
- The force of Earth's gravity on a human being with a mass of 70 kg is approximately 687 N.
- The dot product of force and distance is mechanical work. Thus, in SI units, a force of 1 N exerted over a distance of 1 m is 1 N·m of work. The Work-Energy Theorem states that the work done on a body is equal to the change in energy of the body. 1 N·m = 1 J (joule), the SI unit of energy.
- It is common to see forces expressed in kilonewtons or kN, where 1 kN = 1 000 N.

a. 1-center problem
b. 2-3 heap
c. Newton
d. 120-cell

15. In abstract algebra, a module S over a ring R is called _____ or irreducible if it is not the zero module 0 and if its only submodules are 0 and S. Understanding the _____ modules over a ring is usually helpful because these modules form the 'building blocks' of all other modules in a certain sense.

Abelian groups are the same as Z-modules.

a. Derivation
b. Basis
c. Harmonic series
d. Simple

16. In linear algebra, _____ is an efficient algorithm for solving systems of linear equations, finding the rank of a matrix, and calculating the inverse of an invertible square matrix. _____ is named after German mathematician and scientist Carl Friedrich Gauss.

Elementary row operations are used to reduce a matrix to row echelon form.

a. Crout matrix decomposition
b. Cholesky decomposition
c. Conjugate gradient method
d. Gaussian elimination

17. In chemistry, _____ is the measure of how much of a given substance there is mixed with another substance. This can apply to any sort of chemical mixture, but most frequently the concept is limited to homogeneous solutions, where it refers to the amount of solute in the solvent.

To concentrate a solution, one must add more solute, or reduce the amount of solvent (for instance, by selective evaporation.)

Chapter 2. Solutions of Equations of One Variable

a. 120-cell
b. 2-3 heap
c. 1-center problem
d. Concentration

18. In mathematics, two vectors are _____ if they are perpendicular. For example, a subway and the street above, although they do not physically intersect, are _____ if they cross at a right angle.
a. Orthogonal
b. Algebraic structure
c. Additive identity
d. Unique factorization domain

19. The multiple integral is a type of definite integral extended to functions of more than one real variable, for example, fz = x^2 + y^2. The rectangular region at the bottom of the body is the domain of integration, while the surface is the graph of the two-variable function to be integrated.

Introduction

Just as the definite integral of a positive function of one variable represents the area of the region between the graph of the function and the x-axis, the _____ of a positive function of two variables represents the volume of the region between the surface defined by the function and the plane which contains its domain.

a. Double Integral
b. Signed measure
c. Solid of revolution
d. Risch algorithm

20. In mathematics, the idea of _____ has come to stand for a very general idea, extending the intuitive idea of 'gluing' in topology. Since the topologists' glue is actually the use of equivalence relations on topological spaces, the theory starts with some ideas on identification.

A sophisticated theory resulted.

a. Dominance
b. Deviance
c. Block size
d. Descent

21. In applied mathematics and mechanical engineering, the _____ is a widely used, classical method for the calculation of the natural vibration frequency of a structure in the second or higher order. It is a direct variational method in which the minimum of a functional defined on a normed linear space is approximated by a linear combination of elements from that space. This method will yield solutions when an analytical form for the true solution may be intractable.
a. 2-3 heap
b. 1-center problem
c. Rayleigh-Ritz method
d. 120-cell

22. In mathematics, the _____s are analogs of the ordinary trigonometric functions. The basic _____s are the hyperbolic sine 'sinh', and the hyperbolic cosine 'cosh', from which are derived the hyperbolic tangent 'tanh', etc., in analogy to the derived trigonometric functions. The inverse _____ are the area hyperbolic sine 'arsinh' (also called 'asinh', or sometimes by the misnomer of 'arcsinh') and so on.
a. Square root
b. Heaviside step function
c. Rectangular function
d. Hyperbolic function

23. In common usage, a cylinder is taken to mean a finite section of a right _____ with its ends closed to form two circular surfaces, as in the figure (right.) If the cylinder has a radius r and length (height) h, then its volume is given by

$$V = \pi r^2 h$$

and its surface area is:

- the area of the top (πr^2) +
- the area of the bottom (πr^2) +
- the area of the side $(2\pi rh)$.

Therefore without the top or bottom (lateral area), the surface area is

$$A = 2\pi rh.$$

With the top and bottom, the surface area is

$$A = 2\pi r^2 + 2\pi rh = 2\pi r(r+h).$$

For a given volume, the cylinder with the smallest surface area has h = 2r. For a given surface area, the cylinder with the largest volume has h = 2r, i.e. the cylinder fits in a cube (height = diameter.)

Cylindric sections are the intersections of cylinders with planes.

a. Circular cylinder
c. 1-center problem

b. 120-cell
d. 2-3 heap

24. In mathematics, a _____ is a quadric surface, with the following equation in Cartesian coordinates: $(x/_a)^2 + (y/_b)^2 = 1$.

a. Derivative algebra
c. Free

b. Discontinuity
d. Cylinder

25. In mathematics, a _____ is a rectangular table of elements, which may be numbers or, more generally, any abstract quantities that can be added and multiplied. Matrices are used to describe linear equations, keep track of the coefficients of linear transformations and to record data that depend on multiple parameters. Matrices are described by the field of _____ theory.

a. Double counting
c. Compression

b. Coherent
d. Matrix

26. In linear algebra, functional analysis and related areas of mathematics, a _____ is a function that assigns a strictly positive length or size to all vectors in a vector space, other than the zero vector. A seminorm, on the other hand, is allowed to assign zero length to some non-zero vectors.

A simple example is the 2-dimensional Euclidean space R^2 equipped with the Euclidean _____.

a. Going up
b. Leibniz formula
c. Compression
d. Norm

27. Leonardo of Pisa (c. 1170 - c. 1250), also known as Leonardo Pisano, Leonardo Bonacci, Leonardo _____, or, most commonly, simply _____, was an Italian mathematician, considered by some 'the most talented mathematician of the Middle Ages'.
   a. Guido Castelnuovo
   b. Harry Hinsley
   c. Ralph C. Merkle
   d. Fibonacci

Chapter 3. Interpolation and Polynomial Approximation

1. In mathematical analysis, the _____ states that for each value between the least upper bound and greatest lower bound of the image of a continuous function there is a corresponding value in its domain mapping to the original. _____

   - Version I. The _____ states the following: If the function y = f∈ [a, b] such that f

   - Version II. Suppose that I is an interval [a, b] in the real numbers R and that f : I → R is a continuous function. Then the image set f

     f⊇ [f or f(I) ⊇ [f(b), f(a)].

   It is frequently stated in the following equivalent form: Suppose that f : [a, b] → R is continuous and that u is a real number satisfying f(a) < u < f(b) or f(a) > u > f(b.) Then for some c ∈ [a, b], f(c) = u.

   This captures an intuitive property of continuous functions: given f continuous on [1, 2], if f(1) = 3 and f(2) = 5 then f must take the value 4 somewhere between 1 and 2.

   a. Intermediate Value Theorem
   b. Uniformly continuous
   c. A Mathematical Theory of Communication
   d. Equicontinuous

2. In mathematics, a _____ is a statement that can be proved on the basis of explicitly stated or previously agreed assumptions.

   a. Boolean function
   b. Theorem
   c. Logical value
   d. Disjunction introduction

3. In mathematical analysis, the _____ states that every continuous function defined on an interval [a,b] can be uniformly approximated as closely as desired by a polynomial function. Because polynomials are the simplest functions, and computers can directly evaluate polynomials, this theorem has both practical and theoretical relevance, especially in polynomial interpolation. The original version of this result was established by Karl Weierstrass in 1885.

   a. Weierstrass Approximation Theorem
   b. Peano curve
   c. Tietze extension theorem
   d. Space-filling curve

4. In mathematics, a _____ is an expression constructed from variables and constants, using the operations of addition, subtraction, multiplication, and constant non-negative whole number exponents. For example, $x^2 - 4x + 7$ is a _____, but $x^2 - 4/x + 7x^{3/2}$ is not, because its second term involves division by the variable x and also because its third term contains an exponent that is not a whole number.

   _____s are one of the most important concepts in algebra and throughout mathematics and science.

   a. Polynomial
   b. Semifield
   c. Coimage
   d. Group extension

5. In mathematics, a _____ is a system which is not linear. Less technically, a _____ is any problem where the variabl to be solved for cannot be written as a linear sum of independent components. A nonhomogenous system, which is linear apart from the presence of a function of the independent variables, is nonlinear according to a strict definition, but such systems are usually studied alongside linear systems, because they can be transformed to a linear system as long as a particular solution is known.

Chapter 3. Interpolation and Polynomial Approximation

a. 1-center problem
c. Metric system
b. George Dantzig
d. Nonlinear system

6. The _____ Evaluation and Review Technique, commonly abbreviated PERT, is a model for project management designed to analyze and represent the tasks involved in completing a given project.

PERT is a method to analyze the involved tasks in completing a given project, especially the time needed to complete each task, and identifying the minimum time needed to complete the total project.

This model was invented by Booz Allen Hamilton, Inc.

a. Battle of the Sexes
c. Key server
b. Huge
d. Program

7. In mathematics and in the sciences, a _____ (plural: _____e, formulæ or _____s) is a concise way of expressing information symbolically (as in a mathematical or chemical _____), or a general relationship between quantities. One of many famous _____e is Albert Einstein's E = mc² (see special relativity

In mathematics, a _____ is a key to solve an equation with variables. For example, the problem of determining the volume of a sphere is one that requires a significant amount of integral calculus to solve.

a. 1-center problem
c. Formula
b. 120-cell
d. 2-3 heap

8. _____ is a method of constructing new data points from a discrete set of known data points.
a. Archimedes' use of infinitesimals
c. Integration by substitution
b. Uniform convergence
d. Interpolation

9. In the mathematical subfield of numerical analysis, _____ is the interpolation of a given data set by a polynomial. In other words, given some data points (such as obtained by sampling), the aim is to find a polynomial which goes exactly through these points.

Polynomials can be used to approximate more complicated curves, for example, the shapes of letters in typography, given a few points.

a. Linear predictive analysis
c. Newton polynomial
b. Pareto interpolation
d. Polynomial interpolation

10. In mathematics, _____, first defined by the mathematician Daniel Bernoulli and generalized by Friedrich Bessel, are canonical solutions ys differential equation:

$$x^2 \frac{d^2 y}{dx^2} + x \frac{dy}{dx} + (x^2 - \alpha^2)y = 0$$

Chapter 3. Interpolation and Polynomial Approximation

for an arbitrary real or complex number α. The most common and important special case is where α is an integer n.

Although α and −α produce the same differential equation, it is conventional to define different _____ for these two orders.

a. Mittag-Leffler function
b. Jack function
c. Legendre chi function
d. Bessel functions

11. The mathematical concept of a _____ expresses the intuitive idea of deterministic dependence between two quantities, one of which is viewed as primary and the other as secondary. A _____ then is a way to associate a unique output for each input of a specified type, for example, a real number or an element of a given set.

a. Grill
b. Function
c. Going up
d. Coherent

12. The _____, is achieved in a packed stadium when successive groups of spectators briefly stand and raise their arms. Each spectator is required to rise at the same time as those straight in front and behind, and slightly after the person immediately to either the right or the left. Immediately upon stretching to full height, the spectator returns to the usual seated position.

a. Lagrangian
b. Wave
c. Pauli exclusion principle
d. Thermodynamic limit

13. The _____ is an important second-order linear partial differential equation that describes the propagation of a variety of waves, such as sound waves, light waves and water waves. It arises in fields such as acoustics, electromagnetics, and fluid dynamics. Historically, the problem of a vibrating string such as that of a musical instrument was studied by Jean le Rond d'Alembert, Leonhard Euler, Daniel Bernoulli, and Joseph-Louis Lagrange.

a. Wave Equation
b. Random walk
c. Lagrangian
d. Cauchy momentum equation

14. The _____ item is the initial item of a zero-based sequence (that is, a sequence which is numbered beginning from zero rather than one), such as the non-negative integers (see natural number.)

This kind of numbering is common in array references in computer systems, so hackers, computer scientists and computer professionals often use _____ where others might use first, and so forth. Although there is logical reasoning for this (explained below) in programming and mathematics, there is little logical reasoning to use this in other areas, yet it often is.

a. Successor ordinal
b. Zeroth
c. Limit ordinal
d. Transfinite induction

15. The _____ (symbol: N) is the SI derived unit of force, named after Isaac _____ in recognition of his work on classical mechanics.

The _____ is the unit of force derived in the SI system; it is equal to the amount of force required to accelerate a mass of one kilogram at a rate of one meter per second per second. Algebraically:

Chapter 3. Interpolation and Polynomial Approximation 21

$$1\ N = 1\ \frac{kg \cdot m}{s^2}.$$

- 1 N is the force of Earth's gravity on an object with a mass of about 102 g ($1/_{9.8}$ kg) (such as a small apple.)
- On Earth's surface, a mass of 1 kg exerts a force of approximately 9.80665 N [down] (or 1 kgf.) The approximation of 1 kg corresponding to 10 N is sometimes used as a rule of thumb in everyday life and in engineering.
- The force of Earth's gravity on a human being with a mass of 70 kg is approximately 687 N.
- The dot product of force and distance is mechanical work. Thus, in SI units, a force of 1 N exerted over a distance of 1 m is 1 NÂ·m of work. The Work-Energy Theorem states that the work done on a body is equal to the change in energy of the body. 1 NÂ·m = 1 J (joule), the SI unit of energy.
- It is common to see forces expressed in kilonewtons or kN, where 1 kN = 1 000 N.

a. Newton
b. 2-3 heap
c. 120-cell
d. 1-center problem

16. In the mathematical subfield of numerical analysis, a _____ is a spline function that has minimal support with respect to a given degree, smoothness, and domain partition. A fundamental theorem states that every spline function of a given degree, smoothness, and domain partition, can be represented as a linear combination of _____s of that same degree and smoothness, and over that same partition. The term _____ was coined by Isaac Jacob Schoenberg and is short for basis spline.

a. Non-uniform rational B-spline
b. Cubic Hermite spline
c. 1-center problem
d. B-spline

17. The multiple integral is a type of definite integral extended to functions of more than one real variable, for example, fz = x^2 + y^2. The rectangular region at the bottom of the body is the domain of integration, while the surface is the graph of the two-variable function to be integrated.

Introduction

Just as the definite integral of a positive function of one variable represents the area of the region between the graph of the function and the x-axis, the _____ of a positive function of two variables represents the volume of the region between the surface defined by the function and the plane which contains its domain.

a. Signed measure
b. Double Integral
c. Risch algorithm
d. Solid of revolution

18. In commutative algebra, the notions of an element _____ over a ring, and of an _____ extension of rings, are a generalization of the notions in field theory of an element being algebraic over a field, and of an algebraic extension of fields.

The special case of greatest interest in number theory is that of complex numbers _____ over the ring of integers Z.

The term ring will be understood to mean commutative ring with a unit.

a. Integral test for convergence
c. Integral

b. Antidifferentiation
d. Arc length

19. In mathematics, the _____ s are a classical orthogonal polynomial sequence that arise in probability, such as the Edgeworth series; in combinatorics, as an example of an Appell sequence, obeying the umbral calculus; and in physics, where they give rise to the eigenstates of the quantum harmonic oscillator. They are named in honor of Charles Hermite.

The _____ s are defined either by

$$H_n(x) = (-1)^n e^{x^2/2} \frac{d^n}{dx^n} e^{-x^2/2}$$

(the 'probabilists' _____ s'), or sometimes by

$$H_n(x) = (-1)^n e^{x^2} \frac{d^n}{dx^n} e^{-x^2}$$

(the 'physicists' _____ s'.)

a. 1-center problem
c. Hermite polynomial

b. 120-cell
d. 2-3 heap

20. _____ is a fundamental construction of differential calculus and admits many possible generalizations within the fields of mathematical analysis, combinatorics, algebra, and geometry.

In real, complex, and functional analysis, _____ s are generalized to functions of several real or complex variables and functions between topological vector spaces. An important case is the variational _____ in the calculus of variations.

a. Derivative
c. Functional derivative

b. Lin-Tsien equation
d. Metric derivative

21. _____ is a method closely related to the Newton divided difference method of interpolation in numerical analysis, that allows us to consider given derivatives at data points, as well as the data points themselves. The interpolation will give a polynomial that has a degree less than or equal to the number of both data points and their derivatives, minus 1.

The derivatives are treated as extra points, and in the divided difference table, the points are repeated.

Chapter 3. Interpolation and Polynomial Approximation

a. Simple rational approximation
c. Hermite interpolation
b. Padua point
d. Nearest-neighbor interpolation

22. In applied mathematics and mechanical engineering, the _____ is a widely used, classical method for the calculation of the natural vibration frequency of a structure in the second or higher order. It is a direct variational method in which the minimum of a functional defined on a normed linear space is approximated by a linear combination of elements from that space. This method will yield solutions when an analytical form for the true solution may be intractable.
   a. Rayleigh-Ritz method
   c. 1-center problem
   b. 2-3 heap
   d. 120-cell

23. In mathematics, the _____ is an integral equation whose solution gives rise to Fredholm theory, the study of Fredholm kernels and Fredholm operators. The integral equation was studied by Ivar Fredholm.

A homogeneous Fredholm equation of the first kind is written as:

$$g(t) = \int_a^b K(t,s) f(s)\, ds$$

and the problem is, given the continuous kernel function , and the function , to find the function .

   a. Liouville-Neumann series
   c. Fredholm integral equation
   b. Fredholm kernel
   d. Fredholm operator

24. _____ is a finite element analysis (FEA) program that was originally developed for NASA in the late 1960s under United States government funding for the Aerospace industry. The MacNeal-Schwendler Corporation (MSC) was one of the principal and original developers of the public domain _____ code. _____ source code is integrated in a number of different software packages, which are distributed by a range of companies.
   a. Femap
   c. NASTRAN
   b. SAMCEF
   d. LS-DYNA

25. In topology, the _____ of a subset S of a topological space X is the set of points which can be approached both from S and from the outside of S. More formally, it is the set of points in the closure of S, not belonging to the interior of S. An element of the _____ of S is called a _____ point of S.
   a. Character
   c. Heap
   b. Bertrand paradox
   d. Boundary

26. In mathematics, a group G is called _____ if there is a subset S of G such that any element of G can be written in one and only one way as a product of finitely many elements of S and their inverses.

A related but different notion is a _____ abelian group.

_____ groups first arose in the study of hyperbolic geometry, as examples of Fuchsian groups.

a. Leibniz formula
b. Free
c. Barycentric coordinates
d. Boolean algebra

27. In mathematics, an _____ is an equation in which an unknown function appears under an integral sign. There is a close connection between differential and _____s, and some problems may be formulated either way. See, for example, Maxwell's equations.
   a. A Mathematical Theory of Communication
   b. A chemical equation
   c. A posteriori
   d. Integral equation

28. In mathematics, the concept of a _____ tries to capture the intuitive idea of a geometrical one-dimensional and continuous object. A simple example is the circle. In everyday use of the term '_____', a straight line is not curved, but in mathematical parlance _____s include straight lines and line segments.
   a. Curve
   b. Negative pedal curve
   c. Kappa curve
   d. Quadrifolium

29. _____ of class C^r (i.e. γ is r times continuously differentiable) is called a _____ of class C^r or a C^r parametrization of the curve γ. t is called the parameter of the curve γ. γ(I) is called the image of the curve.
   a. Parametric curve
   b. Chern-Weil theory
   c. Geodesic deviation equation
   d. Riemannian connection on a surface

30. In mathematics, particularly linear algebra and numerical analysis, the _____ is a method for orthogonalizing a set of vectors in an inner product space, most commonly the Euclidean space R^n. The _____ takes a finite, linearly independent set S = {v_1, â€¦, v_n} and generates an orthogonal set S' = {u_1, â€¦, u_n} that spans the same subspace as S.

The method is named for J>ørgen Pedersen Gram and Erhard Schmidt but it appeared earlier in the work of Laplace and Cauchy.

   a. Dot product
   b. Homogeneous coordinates
   c. Linear algebra
   d. Gram-Schmidt process

31. In algebra, a _____ of an element in a quadratic extension field of a field K is its image under the unique non-identity automorphism of the extended field that fixes K. If the extension is generated by a square root of an element r of K, then the _____ of $a + b\sqrt{r}$ is $a - b\sqrt{r}$ for $a, b \in K$, and in particular in the case of the field C of complex numbers as an extension of the field R of real numbers, the complex _____ of a + bi is a − bi.

Forming the sum or product of any element of the extension field with its _____ always gives an element of K.

   a. Real structure
   b. Trinomial
   c. Conjugate
   d. Relation algebra

32. In vector calculus, the _____ of a scalar field is a vector field which points in the direction of the greatest rate of increase of the scalar field, and whose magnitude is the greatest rate of change.

A generalization of the _____ for functions on a Euclidean space which have values in another Euclidean space is the Jacobian. A further generalization for a function from one Banach space to another is the Fréchet derivative.

a. Directional derivative
b. Metric derivative
c. Stationary point
d. Gradient

Chapter 4. Numerical Integration and Differentiation

1. The _____ (symbol: N) is the SI derived unit of force, named after Isaac _____ in recognition of his work on classical mechanics.

   The _____ is the unit of force derived in the SI system; it is equal to the amount of force required to accelerate a mass of one kilogram at a rate of one meter per second per second. Algebraically:

   $$1\ N = 1\ \frac{kg \cdot m}{s^2}.$$

   - 1 N is the force of Earth's gravity on an object with a mass of about 102 g ($\frac{1}{9.8}$ kg) (such as a small apple.)
   - On Earth's surface, a mass of 1 kg exerts a force of approximately 9.80665 N [down] (or 1 kgf.) The approximation of 1 kg corresponding to 10 N is sometimes used as a rule of thumb in everyday life and in engineering.
   - The force of Earth's gravity on a human being with a mass of 70 kg is approximately 687 N.
   - The dot product of force and distance is mechanical work. Thus, in SI units, a force of 1 N exerted over a distance of 1 m is 1 N·m of work. The Work-Energy Theorem states that the work done on a body is equal to the change in energy of the body. 1 N·m = 1 J (joule), the SI unit of energy.
   - It is common to see forces expressed in kilonewtons or kN, where 1 kN = 1 000 N.

   a. 2-3 heap
   b. 1-center problem
   c. Newton
   d. 120-cell

2. In mathematics and in the sciences, a _____ (plural: _____e, formulæ or _____s) is a concise way of expressing information symbolically (as in a mathematical or chemical _____), or a general relationship between quantities. One of many famous _____e is Albert Einstein's E = mc² (see special relativity

   In mathematics, a _____ is a key to solve an equation with variables. For example, the problem of determining the volume of a sphere is one that requires a significant amount of integral calculus to solve.

   a. 2-3 heap
   b. 120-cell
   c. 1-center problem
   d. Formula

3. The _____ Evaluation and Review Technique, commonly abbreviated PERT, is a model for project management designed to analyze and represent the tasks involved in completing a given project.

   PERT is a method to analyze the involved tasks in completing a given project, especially the time needed to complete each task, and identifying the minimum time needed to complete the total project.

   This model was invented by Booz Allen Hamilton, Inc.

   a. Key server
   b. Program
   c. Battle of the Sexes
   d. Huge

Chapter 4. Numerical Integration and Differentiation

4. In mathematics, an _____ is a vector space with the additional structure of inner product. This additional structure associates each pair of vectors in the space with a scalar quantity known as the inner product of the vectors. Inner products allow the rigorous introduction of intuitive geometrical notions such as the length of a vector or the angle between two vectors.

   a. Inner product space
   b. A posteriori
   c. A Mathematical Theory of Communication
   d. A chemical equation

5. In commutative algebra, the notions of an element _____ over a ring, and of an _____ extension of rings, are a generalization of the notions in field theory of an element being algebraic over a field, and of an algebraic extension of fields.

The special case of greatest interest in number theory is that of complex numbers _____ over the ring of integers Z.

The term ring will be understood to mean commutative ring with a unit.

   a. Integral
   b. Antidifferentiation
   c. Integral test for convergence
   d. Arc length

6. In statistics, _____ has two related meanings:

- the arithmetic _____.
- the expected value of a random variable, which is also called the population _____.

It is sometimes stated that the '_____' _____s average. This is incorrect if '_____' is taken in the specific sense of 'arithmetic _____' as there are different types of averages: the _____, median, and mode. For instance, average house prices almost always use the median value for the average.

For a real-valued random variable X, the _____ is the expectation of X.

   a. Mean
   b. Proportional hazards model
   c. Statistical population
   d. Probability

7. In calculus, the _____ states, roughly, that given a section of a smooth curve, there is at least one point on that section at which the derivative of the curve is equal to the 'average' derivative of the section. It is used to prove theorems that make global conclusions about a function on an interval starting from local hypotheses about derivatives at points of the interval.

This theorem can be understood concretely by applying it to motion: if a car travels one hundred miles in one hour, so that its average speed during that time was 100 miles per hour, then at some time its instantaneous speed must have been exactly 100 miles per hour.

   a. Fundamental Theorem of Calculus
   b. Functional integration
   c. Calculus controversy
   d. Mean Value Theorem

Chapter 4. Numerical Integration and Differentiation

8. In mathematics, a _____ is a statement that can be proved on the basis of explicitly stated or previously agreed assumptions.
   a. Disjunction introduction
   b. Logical value
   c. Boolean function
   d. Theorem

9. In mathematics, the trapezium rule or _____ is a way to approximately calculate the definite integral

$$\int_a^b f(x)\,dx.$$

The trapezium rule works by approximating the region under the graph of the function f by a trapezium and calculating its area. It follows that

$$\int_a^b f(x)\,dx \approx (b-a)\frac{f(a)+f(b)}{2}.$$

To calculate this integral more accurately, one first splits the interval of integration [a,b] into n smaller subintervals, and then applies the trapezium rule on each of them. One obtains the composite trapezium rule:

$$\int_a^b f(x)\,dx \approx \frac{b-a}{n}\left[\frac{f(a)+f(b)}{2} + \sum_{k=1}^{n-1} f\left(a+k\frac{b-a}{n}\right)\right].$$

This can alternatively be written as:

$$\int_a^b f(x)\,dx \approx \frac{b-a}{2n}\left(f(x_0)+2f(x_1)+2f(x_2)+\cdots+2f(x_{n-1})+f(x_n)\right)$$

where

$$x_k = a + k\frac{b-a}{n}, \text{ for } k=0,1,\ldots,n.$$

   a. 2-3 heap
   b. 120-cell
   c. 1-center problem
   d. Trapezoidal rule

10. A _____ number is a positive integer which has a positive divisor other than one or itself. By definition, every integer greater than one is either a prime number or a _____ number.zero and one are considered to be neither prime nor _____. For example, the integer 14 is a _____ number because it can be factored as 2 × 7.
    a. Basis
    b. Key server
    c. Discontinuity
    d. Composite

11. _____ is a core concept of basic mathematics, specifically in the fields of infinitesimal calculus and mathematical analysis. Given a function f

Chapter 4. Numerical Integration and Differentiation

$$\int_a^b f(x)\,dx,$$

is equal to the area of a region in the xy-plane bounded by the graph of f, the x-axis, and the vertical lines x = a and x = b, with areas below the x-axis being subtracted.

The term 'integral' may also refer to the notion of antiderivative, a function F whose derivative is the given function f.

a. Integration
b. OMAC
c. Apex
d. Epigraph

12. A _____ or a trapezium is a quadrilateral that has at least one pair of parallel lines for sides.

Some authors define it as a quadrilateral having exactly one pair of parallel sides, so as to exclude parallelograms, which otherwise would be regarded as a special type of _____, but most mathematicians use the inclusive definition.

In North America, the term trapezium is used to refer to a quadrilateral with no parallel sides.

a. Lozenge
b. Trapezium
c. Rhomboid
d. Trapezoid

13. A _____ is the difference between the calculated approximation of a number and its exact mathematical value. Numerical analysis specifically tries to estimate this error when using approximation equations and/or algorithms, especially when using finite digits to represent infinite digits of real numbers. This is a form of quantization error.

a. Minimum polynomial extrapolation
b. Large eddy simulation
c. Round-off error
d. Numerical model of the solar system

14. In probability theory and statistics, the _____ of a family of probability distributions is an important property which basically states that if one has a number of random variates that are 'in the family', any linear combination of these variates will also be 'in the family'. Specifically, the family of probability distributions here is a location-scale family, consisting of probability distributions that differ only in location and scale and 'in the family' means that the random variates have a distribution function that is a member of the family.

The importance of a stable family of probability distributions is that they serve as 'attractors' for linear combinations of non-stable random variates.

a. Convergent
b. Stability
c. Torsion
d. Secant

15. The _____ of a material is defined as its mass per unit volume:

$$\rho = \frac{m}{V}$$

Different materials usually have different densities, so _____ is an important concept regarding buoyancy, metal purity and packaging.

In some cases _____ is expressed as the dimensionless quantities specific gravity or relative _____, in which case it is expressed in multiples of the _____ of some other standard material, usually water or air.

In a well-known story, Archimedes was given the task of determining whether King Hiero's goldsmith was embezzling gold during the manufacture of a wreath dedicated to the gods and replacing it with another, cheaper alloy.

a. Density
b. 1-center problem
c. 120-cell
d. 2-3 heap

16. The mathematical concept of a _____ expresses the intuitive idea of deterministic dependence between two quantities, one of which is viewed as primary and the other as secondary. A _____ then is a way to associate a unique output for each input of a specified type, for example, a real number or an element of a given set.
a. Going up
b. Grill
c. Coherent
d. Function

17. In mathematics, specifically in combinatorial commutative algebra, a convex lattice polytope P is called _____ if it has the following property: given any positive integer n, every lattice point of the dilation nP, obtained from P by scaling its vertices by the factor n and taking the convex hull of the resulting points, can be written as the sum of exactly n lattice points in P. This property plays an important role in the theory of toric varieties, where it corresponds to projective normality of the toric variety determined by P.

The simplex in R^k with the vertices at the origin and along the unit coordinate vectors is _____.

a. Demihypercubes
b. Hypercube
c. Polytetrahedron
d. Normal

18. In mathematics, a _____ is an expression constructed from variables and constants, using the operations of addition, subtraction, multiplication, and constant non-negative whole number exponents. For example, $x^2 - 4x + 7$ is a _____, but $x^2 - 4/x + 7x^{3/2}$ is not, because its second term involves division by the variable x and also because its third term contains an exponent that is not a whole number.

_____s are one of the most important concepts in algebra and throughout mathematics and science.

a. Semifield
b. Coimage
c. Polynomial
d. Group extension

Chapter 4. Numerical Integration and Differentiation

19. Augustin-Jean _____ (10 May 1788 - 14 July 1827), was a French physicist who contributed significantly to the establishment of the theory of wave optics. _____ studied the behaviour of light both theoretically and experimentally.

_____ was the son of an architect, born at Broglie (Eure.)

a. Ralph C. Merkle
c. James Dickson Murray
b. Kaisa Nyberg
d. Fresnel

20. _____, S(x) and C(x), are two transcendental functions named after Augustin-Jean Fresnel that are used in optics. They arise in the description of near field Fresnel diffraction phenomena, and are defined through the following integral representations:

$$S(x) = \int_0^x \sin(t^2)\, dt, \quad C(x) = \int_0^x \cos(t^2)\, dt.$$

The simultaneous parametric plot of S(x) and C(x) is the Cornu spiral, or clothoid.

Normalised _____, S(x) and C(x).
a. Spiral
c. Logarithmic spiral
b. Spiral of Theodorus
d. Fresnel integrals

21. _____ is normally taken to refer to various phenomena which occur when a wave encounters an obstacle. It is described as the apparent bending of waves around small obstacles and the spreading out of waves past small openings. Very similar effects are observed when there is an alteration in the properties of the medium in which the wave is travelling, for example a variation in refractive index for light waves or in acoustic impedance for sound waves and these can also be referred to as _____ effects.

a. Wave equation
c. Pauli exclusion principle
b. Vector space
d. Diffraction

22. The _____ is a type of definite integral extended to functions of more than one real variable, for example, fz = x² + y². The rectangular region at the bottom of the body is the domain of integration, while the surface is the graph of the two-variable function to be integrated.

Introduction

Just as the definite integral of a positive function of one variable represents the area of the region between the graph of the function and the x-axis, the double integral of a positive function of two variables represents the volume of the region between the surface defined by the function and the plane which contains its domain.

a. Surface of revolution
c. Multiple integral
b. Solid of revolution
d. Signed measure

23. The multiple integral is a type of definite integral extended to functions of more than one real variable, for example, fz = x² + y². The rectangular region at the bottom of the body is the domain of integration, while the surface is the graph of the two-variable function to be integrated.

Chapter 4. Numerical Integration and Differentiation

Introduction

Just as the definite integral of a positive function of one variable represents the area of the region between the graph of the function and the x-axis, the _____ of a positive function of two variables represents the volume of the region between the surface defined by the function and the plane which contains its domain.

- a. Signed measure
- b. Solid of revolution
- c. Risch algorithm
- d. Double integral

24. In mathematics, the idea of _____ has come to stand for a very general idea, extending the intuitive idea of 'gluing' in topology. Since the topologists' glue is actually the use of equivalence relations on topological spaces, the theory starts with some ideas on identification.

A sophisticated theory resulted.

- a. Dominance
- b. Block size
- c. Deviance
- d. Descent

25. _____ is a quantity expressing the two-dimensional size of a defined part of a surface, typically a region bounded by a closed curve. The term surface _____ refers to the total _____ of the exposed surface of a 3-dimensional solid, such as the sum of the _____s of the exposed sides of a polyhedron. _____ is an important invariant in the differential geometry of surfaces.

- a. Area
- b. A Mathematical Theory of Communication
- c. A chemical equation
- d. A posteriori

26. In mathematics, specifically in topology, a _____ is a two-dimensional manifold. The most familiar examples are those that arise as the boundaries of solid objects in ordinary three-dimensional Euclidean space, EÂ³. On the other hand, there are also more exotic _____s, that are so 'contorted' that they cannot be embedded in three-dimensional space at all.

- a. Cross-cap
- b. Homoeoid
- c. Standard torus
- d. Surface

27. _____ is how much exposed area an object has. It is expressed in square units. If an object has flat faces, its _____ can be calculated by adding together the areas of its faces.

- a. Surface area
- b. Relative dimension
- c. Reflection group
- d. Compactness measure of a shape

28. The Institute of Electrical and Electronics Engineers or _____ (read eye-triple-e) is an international non-profit, professional organization for the advancement of technology related to electricity. It has the most members of any technical professional organization in the world, with more than 365,000 members in around 150 countries.

The _____ is incorporated in the State of New York, United States.

Chapter 4. Numerical Integration and Differentiation

a. IEEE
b. A chemical equation
c. A Mathematical Theory of Communication
d. A posteriori

29. The term _____ or centre is used in various contexts in abstract algebra to denote the set of all those elements that commute with all other elements. More specifically:

- The _____ of a group G consists of all those elements x in G such that xg = gx for all g in G. This is a normal subgroup of G.
- The _____ of a ring R is the subset of R consisting of all those elements x of R such that xr = rx for all r in R. The _____ is a commutative subring of R, so R is an algebra over its _____.
- The _____ of an algebra A consists of all those elements x of A such that xa = ax for all a in A. See also: central simple algebra.
- The _____ of a Lie algebra L consists of all those elements x in L such that [x,a] = 0 for all a in L. This is an ideal of the Lie algebra L.
- The _____ of a monoidal category C consists of pairs *a natural isomorphism satisfying certain axioms*.

a. Brute Force
b. Center
c. Block size
d. Disk

30. The _____ of a system of particles is a specific point at which, for many purposes, the system's mass behaves as if it were concentrated. The _____ is a function only of the positions and masses of the particles that comprise the system. In the case of a rigid body, the position of its _____ is fixed in relation to the object (but not necessarily in contact with it.)

a. Classical mechanics
b. Langevin dynamics
c. Center of mass
d. Friction

31. In calculus, an _____ is the limit of a definite integral as an endpoint of the interval of integration approaches either a specified real number or ∞ or −∞ or, in some cases, as both endpoints approach limits.

Specifically, an _____ is a limit of the form

$$\lim_{b\to\infty} \int_a^b f(x)\,dx, \qquad \lim_{a\to -\infty} \int_a^b f(x)\,dx,$$

or of the form

$$\lim_{c\to b^-} \int_a^c f(x)\,dx, \qquad \lim_{c\to a^+} \int_c^b f(x)\,dx,$$

in which one takes a limit in one or the other endpoints . _____s may also occur at an interior point of the domain of integration, or at multiple such points.

a. Improper integral
b. Elliptic boundary value problem
c. Isoperimetric dimension
d. Infinite product

Chapter 4. Numerical Integration and Differentiation

32. In applied mathematics and mechanical engineering, the _____ is a widely used, classical method for the calculation of the natural vibration frequency of a structure in the second or higher order. It is a direct variational method in which the minimum of a functional defined on a normed linear space is approximated by a linear combination of elements from that space. This method will yield solutions when an analytical form for the true solution may be intractable.
    a. 2-3 heap
    b. 1-center problem
    c. 120-cell
    d. Rayleigh-Ritz method

33. _____ is a fundamental construction of differential calculus and admits many possible generalizations within the fields of mathematical analysis, combinatorics, algebra, and geometry.

    In real, complex, and functional analysis, _____s are generalized to functions of several real or complex variables and functions between topological vector spaces. An important case is the variational _____ in the calculus of variations.

    a. Metric derivative
    b. Functional derivative
    c. Lin-Tsien equation
    d. Derivative

34. In physics, _____ is the speed where the kinetic energy of an object is equal to the magnitude of its gravitational potential energy, as calculated by the equation,

$$U_g = \frac{-Gm_1 m_2}{r}.$$

    It is commonly described as the speed needed to 'break free' from a gravitational field. The term _____ can be considered a misnomer because it is actually a speed rather than a velocity. ' In more technical terms, _____ is a scalar.

    a. Escape velocity
    b. Ecliptic
    c. A chemical equation
    d. A Mathematical Theory of Communication

35. _____ of an object is its speed in a particular direction.
    a. Velocity
    b. Discontinuity
    c. Maxima
    d. Rolle's Theorem

36. In the mathematical subfield of numerical analysis, a _____ is a spline function that has minimal support with respect to a given degree, smoothness, and domain partition. A fundamental theorem states that every spline function of a given degree, smoothness, and domain partition, can be represented as a linear combination of _____s of that same degree and smoothness, and over that same partition. The term _____ was coined by Isaac Jacob Schoenberg and is short for basis spline.
    a. 1-center problem
    b. Non-uniform rational B-spline
    c. Cubic Hermite spline
    d. B-spline

37. _____, a field in mathematics, is the study of how functions change when their inputs change. The primary object of study in _____ is the derivative. A closely related notion is the differential.

a. Geometric function theory
b. Semi-continuity
c. Differential calculus
d. Harmonic analysis

Chapter 5. Numerical Solution of Initial-Value Problems

1. The multiple integral is a type of definite integral extended to functions of more than one real variable, for example, fz = x^2 + y^2. The rectangular region at the bottom of the body is the domain of integration, while the surface is the graph of the two-variable function to be integrated.

Introduction

Just as the definite integral of a positive function of one variable represents the area of the region between the graph of the function and the x-axis, the _____ of a positive function of two variables represents the volume of the region between the surface defined by the function and the plane which contains its domain.

    a. Risch algorithm   b. Double Integral
    c. Signed measure   d. Solid of revolution

2. In commutative algebra, the notions of an element _____ over a ring, and of an _____ extension of rings, are a generalization of the notions in field theory of an element being algebraic over a field, and of an algebraic extension of fields.

The special case of greatest interest in number theory is that of complex numbers _____ over the ring of integers Z.

The term ring will be understood to mean commutative ring with a unit.

    a. Integral   b. Integral test for convergence
    c. Antidifferentiation   d. Arc length

3. Suppose that φ : M → N is a smooth map between smooth manifolds; then the _____ of φ at a point x is, in some sense, the best linear approximation of φ near x. It can be viewed as generalization of the total derivative of ordinary calculus. Explicitly, it is a linear map from the tangent space of M at x to the tangent space of N at φ

    a. Boundary   b. Grill
    c. Concurrent   d. Differential

4. _____s arise in many problems in physics, engineering, etc. The following examples show how to solve _____s in a few simple cases when an exact solution exists.

A separable linear ordinary _____ of the first order has the general form:

$$\frac{dy}{dt} + f(t)y = 0$$

where f is some known function.

    a. Differential equation   b. Nullcline
    c. Nahm equations   d. Homogeneous differential equation

5. The _____ Evaluation and Review Technique, commonly abbreviated PERT, is a model for project management designed to analyze and represent the tasks involved in completing a given project.

Chapter 5. Numerical Solution of Initial-Value Problems

PERT is a method to analyze the involved tasks in completing a given project, especially the time needed to complete each task, and identifying the minimum time needed to complete the total project.

This model was invented by Booz Allen Hamilton, Inc.

a. Program
c. Battle of the Sexes
b. Key server
d. Huge

6. In mathematics, a _____ is a statement that can be proved on the basis of explicitly stated or previously agreed assumptions.
    a. Theorem
    c. Disjunction introduction
    b. Logical value
    d. Boolean function

7. In mathematical analysis, the _____ states that every continuous function defined on an interval [a,b] can be uniformly approximated as closely as desired by a polynomial function. Because polynomials are the simplest functions, and computers can directly evaluate polynomials, this theorem has both practical and theoretical relevance, especially in polynomial interpolation. The original version of this result was established by Karl Weierstrass in 1885.
    a. Peano curve
    c. Space-filling curve
    b. Weierstrass Approximation Theorem
    d. Tietze extension theorem

8. The mathematical term _____ stems from a definition given by Hadamard. He believed that mathematical models of physical phenomena should have the properties that

    1. A solution exists
    2. The solution is unique
    3. The solution depends continuously on the data, in some reasonable topology.

Examples of archetypal _____s include the Dirichlet problem for Laplace's equation, and the heat equation with specified initial conditions. These might be regarded as 'natural' problems in that there are physical processes that solve these problems. By contrast the inverse heat equation, deducing a previous distribution of temperature from final data is not well-posed in that the solution is highly sensitive to changes in the final data.

a. Discretization error
c. Wavelets
b. Wavelet
d. Well-posed problem

9. In mathematics and computational science, the _____, named after Leonhard Euler, is a first order numerical procedure for solving ordinary differential equations with a given initial value. It is the most basic kind of explicit method for numerical integration for ordinary differential equations.

Consider the problem of calculating the shape of an unknown curve which starts at a given point and satisfies a given differential equation.

a. Uniform theory of diffraction
c. Explicit and implicit methods
b. Analytic element method
d. Euler method

Chapter 5. Numerical Solution of Initial-Value Problems

10. In statistics, _____ has two related meanings:

- the arithmetic _____.
- the expected value of a random variable, which is also called the population _____.

It is sometimes stated that the '_____' _____s average. This is incorrect if '_____' is taken in the specific sense of 'arithmetic _____' as there are different types of averages: the _____, median, and mode. For instance, average house prices almost always use the median value for the average.

For a real-valued random variable X, the _____ is the expectation of X.

a. Proportional hazards model
c. Statistical population
b. Probability
d. Mean

11. In calculus, the _____ states, roughly, that given a section of a smooth curve, there is at least one point on that section at which the derivative of the curve is equal to the 'average' derivative of the section. It is used to prove theorems that make global conclusions about a function on an interval starting from local hypotheses about derivatives at points of the interval.

This theorem can be understood concretely by applying it to motion: if a car travels one hundred miles in one hour, so that its average speed during that time was 100 miles per hour, then at some time its instantaneous speed must have been exactly 100 miles per hour.

a. Fundamental Theorem of Calculus
c. Functional integration
b. Calculus controversy
d. Mean Value Theorem

12. In cryptography, _____ is a block cipher designed in 2002 by Jorge Nakahara, Jr., Vincent Rijmen, Bart Preneel, and Joos Vandewalle. _____ is based directly on IDEA and uses the same basic operations.

_____ is actually a family of 3 variant ciphers with block sizes of 64, 96, and 128 bits.

a. Depth
c. Duality
b. Key server
d. Mesh

13. A _____ is a simple shape of Euclidean geometry consisting of those points in a plane which are at a constant distance, called the radius, from a fixed point, called the center. A _____ with center A is sometimes denoted by the symbol A.

A chord of a _____ is a line segment whose two endpoints lie on the _____.

a. Circle
c. Circular segment
b. Circumcircle
d. Malfatti circles

14. _____ is a method closely related to the Newton divided difference method of interpolation in numerical analysis, that allows us to consider given derivatives at data points, as well as the data points themselves. The interpolation will give a polynomial that has a degree less than or equal to the number of both data points and their derivatives, minus 1.

Chapter 5. Numerical Solution of Initial-Value Problems

The derivatives are treated as extra points, and in the divided difference table, the points are repeated.

a. Simple rational approximation
b. Padua point
c. Nearest-neighbor interpolation
d. Hermite interpolation

15. _____ is a method of constructing new data points from a discrete set of known data points.
a. Uniform convergence
b. Integration by substitution
c. Archimedes' use of infinitesimals
d. Interpolation

16. _____ is a method of curve fitting using linear polynomials. It is heavily employed in mathematics (particularly numerical analysis), and numerous applications including computer graphics. It is a simple form of interpolation.
a. Monotone cubic interpolation
b. Linear interpolation
c. Multivariate interpolation
d. Polynomial interpolation

17. In mathematics, a _____ is an expression constructed from variables and constants, using the operations of addition, subtraction, multiplication, and constant non-negative whole number exponents. For example, $x^2 - 4x + 7$ is a _____, but $x^2 - 4/x + 7x^{3/2}$ is not, because its second term involves division by the variable x and also because its third term contains an exponent that is not a whole number.

_____s are one of the most important concepts in algebra and throughout mathematics and science.

a. Polynomial
b. Coimage
c. Semifield
d. Group extension

18. In linear algebra, a _____ is a matrix with the unit fraction elements

$$H_{ij} = \frac{1}{i+j-1}.$$

For example, this is the 5 × 5 _____:

$$H = \begin{bmatrix} 1 & \frac{1}{2} & \frac{1}{3} & \frac{1}{4} & \frac{1}{5} \\ \frac{1}{2} & \frac{1}{3} & \frac{1}{4} & \frac{1}{5} & \frac{1}{6} \\ \frac{1}{3} & \frac{1}{4} & \frac{1}{5} & \frac{1}{6} & \frac{1}{7} \\ \frac{1}{4} & \frac{1}{5} & \frac{1}{6} & \frac{1}{7} & \frac{1}{8} \\ \frac{1}{5} & \frac{1}{6} & \frac{1}{7} & \frac{1}{8} & \frac{1}{9} \end{bmatrix}.$$

The _____ can be regarded as derived from the integral

$$H_{ij} = \int_0^1 x^{i+j-2}\, dx,$$

that is, as a Gramian matrix for powers of x. It is a Hankel matrix.

The Hilbert matrices are canonical examples of ill-conditioned matrices, making them notoriously difficult to use in numerical computation.

a. Generalized minimal residual method
c. Hilbert matrix
b. Triangular matrix
d. Symbolic Cholesky decomposition

19. In mathematics, a _____ is a rectangular table of elements, which may be numbers or, more generally, any abstract quantities that can be added and multiplied. Matrices are used to describe linear equations, keep track of the coefficients of linear transformations and to record data that depend on multiple parameters. Matrices are described by the field of _____ theory.

a. Compression
c. Double counting
b. Coherent
d. Matrix

20. In numerical analysis, a branch of applied mathematics, the _____ is a one-step method for solving the differential equation

$$y'(t) = f(t, y(t)), \quad y(t_0) = y_0$$

numerically, and is given by the formula

$$y_{n+1} = y_n + hf\left(t_n + \frac{h}{2}, y_n + \frac{h}{2}f(t_n, y_n)\right), \quad (1)$$

for $n = 0, 1, 2, \ldots$ Here, h is the step size -- a small positive number, $t_n = t_0 + nh$, and y_n is the computed approximate value of $y(t_n)$.

The name of the method comes from the fact that in the formula above the function f is evaluated at $t = t_n + h/2$, which is the midpoint between t_n at which the value of y(t) is known and t_{n+1} at which the value of y(t) needs to be found.

The error at each step of the _____ is of order $O\left(h^3\right)$. Thus, while more computationally intensive than Euler's method, the _____ generally gives more accurate results.

The method is an example of a class of higher-order methods known as Runge-Kutta methods.

a. Geometric integrator
c. Discontinuous Galerkin methods
b. Direct multiple shooting method
d. Midpoint method

21. In mathematics, an _____ in the sense of ring theory is a subring $\mathcal{O}$ of a ring R that satisfies the conditions

1. R is a ring which is a finite-dimensional algebra over the rational number field $\mathbb{Q}$
2. $\mathcal{O}$ spans R over $\mathbb{Q}$, so that $\mathbb{Q}\mathcal{O} = R$, and
3. $\mathcal{O}$ is a lattice in R.

Chapter 5. Numerical Solution of Initial-Value Problems

The third condition can be stated more accurately, in terms of the extension of scalars of R to the real numbers, embedding R in a real vector space. In less formal terms, additively $\mathcal{O}$ should be a free abelian group generated by a basis for R over $\mathbb{Q}$.

The leading example is the case where R is a number field K and $\mathcal{O}$ is its ring of integers. In algebraic number theory there are examples for any K other than the rational field of proper subrings of the ring of integers that are also _____s.

a. Efficiency
b. Annihilator
c. Order
d. Algebraic

22. In linear algebra, functional analysis and related areas of mathematics, a _____ is a function that assigns a strictly positive length or size to all vectors in a vector space, other than the zero vector. A seminorm, on the other hand, is allowed to assign zero length to some non-zero vectors.

A simple example is the 2-dimensional Euclidean space R^2 equipped with the Euclidean _____.

a. Leibniz formula
b. Going up
c. Norm
d. Compression

23. The mathematical concept of a _____ expresses the intuitive idea of deterministic dependence between two quantities, one of which is viewed as primary and the other as secondary. A _____ then is a way to associate a unique output for each input of a specified type, for example, a real number or an element of a given set.

a. Going up
b. Grill
c. Coherent
d. Function

24. A _____ is a process that always results in the interconversion of chemical substances. The substance or substances initially involved in a _____ are called reactants. _____s are usually characterized by a chemical change, and they yield one or more products, which usually have properties different from the reactants.

a. 120-cell
b. 2-3 heap
c. 1-center problem
d. Chemical reaction

25. The Institute of Electrical and Electronics Engineers or _____ (read eye-triple-e) is an international non-profit, professional organization for the advancement of technology related to electricity. It has the most members of any technical professional organization in the world, with more than 365,000 members in around 150 countries.

The _____ is incorporated in the State of New York, United States.

a. A posteriori
b. A chemical equation
c. A Mathematical Theory of Communication
d. IEEE

26. In applied mathematics, explicit and implicit methods are approaches used in computer simulations of physical processes they are numerical methods for solving time-variable ordinary and partial differential equations.

Chapter 5. Numerical Solution of Initial-Value Problems

_____s calculate the state of a system at a later time from the state of the system at the current time, while an implicit method finds it by solving an equation involving both the current state of the system and the later one.

a. Explicit method
b. Analytic element method
c. Explicit and implicit methods
d. Uniform theory of diffraction

27. In applied mathematics, explicit and _____s are approaches used in computer simulations of physical processes they are numerical methods for solving time-variable ordinary and partial differential equations.

Explicit methods calculate the state of a system at a later time from the state of the system at the current time, while an _____ finds it by solving an equation involving both the current state of the system and the later one. Mathematically, if Y is the current system state and Y is the state at the later time, then, for an explicit method

$$Y(t + \Delta t) = F(Y(t))$$

while for an _____ one solves an equation

$$G(Y(t), Y(t + \Delta t)) = 0 \quad (1)$$

to find Y

It is clear that _____s require an extra computation, and they can be much harder to implement.

a. Explicit method
b. Euler-Maruyama method
c. Implicit method
d. Explicit and implicit methods

28. In mathematics, particularly numerical analysis, a _____ is an algorithm that proceeds in two steps. First, the prediction step calculates a rough approximation of the desired quantity. Second, the corrector step refines the initial approximation using another means.
a. Well-behaved
b. Plugging in
c. Per mil
d. Predictor-corrector method

29. A _____ number is a positive integer which has a positive divisor other than one or itself. By definition, every integer greater than one is either a prime number or a _____ number.zero and one are considered to be neither prime nor _____. For example, the integer 14 is a _____ number because it can be factored as 2 × 7.
a. Discontinuity
b. Basis
c. Key server
d. Composite

30. In numerical analysis, _____ is a sequence acceleration method, used to improve the rate of convergence of a sequence. It is named after Lewis Fry Richardson, who introduced the technique in the early 20th century. In the words of Birkhoff and Rota, '...

Chapter 5. Numerical Solution of Initial-Value Problems

a. Truncation error
b. Richardson extrapolation
c. Cascade algorithm
d. Constructions of low-discrepancy sequences

31. _____ is the change in population over time, and can be quantified as the change in the number of individuals in a population using 'per unit time' for measurement. The term _____ can technically refer to any species, but almost always refers to humans, and it is often used informally for the more specific demographic term _____ rate, and is often used to refer specifically to the growth of the population of the world.

Simple models of _____ include the Malthusian Growth Model and the logistic model.

a. 1-center problem
b. 120-cell
c. Population growth
d. Population dynamics

32. In ecology, _____ describes a biological interaction where a predator (an organism that is hunting) feeds on its prey, the organism that is attacked. Predators may or may not kill their prey prior to feeding on them, but the act of _____ always results in the death of the prey. The other main category of consumption is detritivory, the consumption of dead organic material (detritus.)

a. Predator
b. 120-cell
c. 1-center problem
d. Predation

33. _____ is a differential equation for which certain numerical methods for solving the equation are numerically unstable, unless the step size is taken to be extremely small.

a. 120-cell
b. 1-center problem
c. 2-3 heap
d. Stiff differential equation

34. The _____ (symbol: N) is the SI derived unit of force, named after Isaac _____ in recognition of his work on classical mechanics.

The _____ is the unit of force derived in the SI system; it is equal to the amount of force required to accelerate a mass of one kilogram at a rate of one meter per second per second. Algebraically:

$$1\text{ N} = 1\ \frac{\text{kg} \cdot \text{m}}{\text{s}^2}.$$

- 1 N is the force of Earth's gravity on an object with a mass of about 102 g ($1/_{9.8}$ kg) (such as a small apple.)
- On Earth's surface, a mass of 1 kg exerts a force of approximately 9.80665 N [down] (or 1 kgf.) The approximation of 1 kg corresponding to 10 N is sometimes used as a rule of thumb in everyday life and in engineering.
- The force of Earth's gravity on a human being with a mass of 70 kg is approximately 687 N.
- The dot product of force and distance is mechanical work. Thus, in SI units, a force of 1 N exerted over a distance of 1 m is 1 N·m of work. The Work-Energy Theorem states that the work done on a body is equal to the change in energy of the body. 1 N·m = 1 J (joule), the SI unit of energy.
- It is common to see forces expressed in kilonewtons or kN, where 1 kN = 1 000 N.

a. 120-cell
c. 1-center problem

b. 2-3 heap
d. Newton

35. In mathematics, a _____ is a differential equation for which certain numerical methods for solving the equation are numerically unstable, unless the step size is taken to be extremely small. It has proven difficult to formulate a precise definition of stiffness, but the main idea is that the equation includes some terms that can lead to rapid variation in the solution.

Consider the initial value problem

$$y'(t) = -15y(t), \quad t \geq 0, y(0) = 1.$$

The exact solution is y− 15t, and clearly y → 0 as t → ∞.

a. High-resolution scheme
c. Numerical diffusion

b. Direct multiple shooting method
d. Stiff equation

Chapter 6. Direct Methods for Solving Linear Systems

1. The multiple integral is a type of definite integral extended to functions of more than one real variable, for example, fz = x^2 + y^2. The rectangular region at the bottom of the body is the domain of integration, while the surface is the graph of the two-variable function to be integrated.

Introduction

Just as the definite integral of a positive function of one variable represents the area of the region between the graph of the function and the x-axis, the _____ of a positive function of two variables represents the volume of the region between the surface defined by the function and the plane which contains its domain.

a. Solid of revolution
b. Risch algorithm
c. Signed measure
d. Double Integral

2. In commutative algebra, the notions of an element _____ over a ring, and of an _____ extension of rings, are a generalization of the notions in field theory of an element being algebraic over a field, and of an algebraic extension of fields.

The special case of greatest interest in number theory is that of complex numbers _____ over the ring of integers Z.

The term ring will be understood to mean commutative ring with a unit.

a. Integral
b. Arc length
c. Antidifferentiation
d. Integral test for convergence

3. The _____ Evaluation and Review Technique, commonly abbreviated PERT, is a model for project management designed to analyze and represent the tasks involved in completing a given project.

PERT is a method to analyze the involved tasks in completing a given project, especially the time needed to complete each task, and identifying the minimum time needed to complete the total project.

This model was invented by Booz Allen Hamilton, Inc.

a. Program
b. Key server
c. Battle of the Sexes
d. Huge

4. A _____ is an algebraic equation in which each term is either a constant or the product of a constant and a single variable. _____s can have one, two, three or more variables.

_____s occur with great regularity in applied mathematics.

a. Difference of two squares
b. Linear equation
c. Quartic equation
d. Quadratic equation

5. In statistics, and particularly in econometrics, the _____ of a system of equations is the result of solving the system for the endogenous variables. This gives the latter as a function of the exogenous variables, if any.

Let Y and X be random vectors.

a. Reduced form
b. Log-linear
c. Test for structural change
d. Dynamic factor

6. In the mathematical discipline of linear algebra, a _____ is a special kind of square matrix where the entries either below or above the main diagonal are zero. Because matrix equations with triangular matrices are easier to solve they are very important in numerical analysis. The LU decomposition gives an algorithm to decompose any invertible matrix A into a normed lower triangle matrix L and an upper triangle matrix U.

a. Rayleigh quotient iteration
b. Crout matrix decomposition
c. Triangular matrix
d. Successive over-relaxation

7. In physics and in _____ calculus, a _____ is a concept characterized by a magnitude and a direction. A _____ can be thought of as an arrow in Euclidean space, drawn from an initial point A pointing to a terminal point B.

a. Dominance
b. Constraint
c. Deviation
d. Vector

8. In linear algebra, the _____ of a matrix is obtained by changing a matrix in some way.

Given the matrices A and B, where:

$$A = \begin{bmatrix} 1 & 3 & 2 \\ 2 & 0 & 1 \\ 5 & 2 & 2 \end{bmatrix}, \quad B = \begin{bmatrix} 4 \\ 3 \\ 1 \end{bmatrix}$$

Then, the _____ is written as:

$$(A|B) = \begin{bmatrix} 1 & 3 & 2 & 4 \\ 2 & 0 & 1 & 3 \\ 5 & 2 & 2 & 1 \end{bmatrix}$$

This is useful when solving systems of linear equations or the _____ may also be used to find the inverse of a matrix by combining it with the identity matrix.

$$C = \begin{bmatrix} 1 & 3 \\ -5 & 0 \end{bmatrix}$$

Let C be a square 2×2 matrix where

To find the inverse of C we create where I is the 2×2 identity matrix.

a. Unimodular polynomial matrix
b. Eigendecomposition
c. Alternating sign matrix
d. Augmented matrix

Chapter 6. Direct Methods for Solving Linear Systems

9. In mathematics, a _____ is a rectangular table of elements, which may be numbers or, more generally, any abstract quantities that can be added and multiplied. Matrices are used to describe linear equations, keep track of the coefficients of linear transformations and to record data that depend on multiple parameters. Matrices are described by the field of _____ theory.

   a. Compression
   b. Coherent
   c. Double counting
   d. Matrix

10. In the mathematical subfield of numerical analysis, a _____ is a spline function that has minimal support with respect to a given degree, smoothness, and domain partition. A fundamental theorem states that every spline function of a given degree, smoothness, and domain partition, can be represented as a linear combination of _____s of that same degree and smoothness, and over that same partition. The term _____ was coined by Isaac Jacob Schoenberg and is short for basis spline.

    a. Cubic Hermite spline
    b. Non-uniform rational B-spline
    c. 1-center problem
    d. B-spline

11. In linear algebra, _____ is an efficient algorithm for solving systems of linear equations, finding the rank of a matrix, and calculating the inverse of an invertible square matrix. _____ is named after German mathematician and scientist Carl Friedrich Gauss.

Elementary row operations are used to reduce a matrix to row echelon form.

   a. Crout matrix decomposition
   b. Gaussian elimination
   c. Conjugate gradient method
   d. Cholesky decomposition

12. In applied mathematics and mechanical engineering, the _____ is a widely used, classical method for the calculation of the natural vibration frequency of a structure in the second or higher order. It is a direct variational method in which the minimum of a functional defined on a normed linear space is approximated by a linear combination of elements from that space. This method will yield solutions when an analytical form for the true solution may be intractable.

    a. 1-center problem
    b. 120-cell
    c. 2-3 heap
    d. Rayleigh-Ritz method

13. In mathematics, an _____ or member of a set is any one of the distinct objects that make up that set.

Writing A = {1,2,3,4}, means that the _____s of the set A are the numbers 1, 2, 3 and 4. Groups of _____s of A, for example {1,2}, are subsets of A.

   a. Ideal
   b. Universal code
   c. Order
   d. Element

14. A _____ is a mathematical model of a system based on the use of a linear operator. _____s typically exhibit features and properties that are much simpler than the general, nonlinear case. As a mathematical abstraction or idealization, _____s find important applications in automatic control theory, signal processing, and telecommunications.

    a. Predispositioning Theory
    b. Percolation
    c. Hybrid system
    d. Linear system

Chapter 6. Direct Methods for Solving Linear Systems

15. In Fourier analysis, a _____ is a kind of linear operator, or transformation of functions. These operators multiply the Fourier coefficients of a function by a specified function, hence the name. Among the multipliers one can count some simple operators, such as translations and differentiation, but also some more complicated ones such as the convolutions, Hilbert transform, and others.
    a. Reality condition
    b. Modulated complex lapped transform
    c. Poisson summation formula
    d. Fourier multiplier

16. In mathematics, the _____ is an integral equation whose solution gives rise to Fredholm theory, the study of Fredholm kernels and Fredholm operators. The integral equation was studied by Ivar Fredholm.

    A homogeneous Fredholm equation of the first kind is written as:

    $$g(t) = \int_a^b K(t,s) f(s)\, ds$$

    and the problem is, given the continuous kernel function , and the function , to find the function .

    a. Fredholm integral equation
    b. Liouville-Neumann series
    c. Fredholm operator
    d. Fredholm kernel

17. In mathematics, an _____ is an equation in which an unknown function appears under an integral sign. There is a close connection between differential and _____s, and some problems may be formulated either way. See, for example, Maxwell's equations.
    a. A posteriori
    b. A chemical equation
    c. A Mathematical Theory of Communication
    d. Integral equation

18. In the case of Gaussian elimination, it is best to choose a pivot element with large absolute value. This improves the numerical stability. In _____, the algorithm considers all entries in the column of the matrix that is currently being considered, picks the entry with largest absolute value, and finally swaps rows such that this entry is the pivot in question.
    a. 2-3 heap
    b. 120-cell
    c. 1-center problem
    d. Partial Pivoting

19. _____ is a branch of mathematics which focuses on the study of matrices. Initially a sub-branch of linear algebra, it has grown to cover subjects related to graph theory, algebra, combinatorics, and statistics as well.

    The term matrix was first coined in 1848 by J.J. Sylvester as a name of an array of numbers.

    a. Semi-simple operators
    b. Segre classification
    c. Pairing
    d. Matrix theory

20. In mathematics, _____ is the operation of adding two matrices by adding the corresponding entries together. However, there is another operation which could also be considered as a kind of addition for matrices.

    The usual _____ is defined for two matrices of the same dimensions.

a. Standard basis
c. Jordan normal form
b. Matrix addition
d. Spectral theory

21. _____ is the mathematical operation of scaling one number by another. It is one of the four basic operations in elementary arithmetic.

_____ is defined for whole numbers in terms of repeated addition; for example, 4 multiplied by 3 can be calculated by adding 3 copies of 4 together:

$$4 + 4 + 4 = 12.$$

_____ of rational numbers and real numbers is defined by systematic generalization of this basic idea.

a. The number 0 is even.
c. Least common multiple
b. Highest common factor
d. Multiplication

22. In mathematics, _____ is one of the basic operations defining a vector space in linear algebra. Note that _____ is different from scalar product which is an inner product between two vectors.

More specifically, if K is a field and V is a vector space over K, then _____ is a function from K × V to V.

a. Non-negative matrix factorization
c. Jordan normal form
b. Scalar multiplication
d. Frobenius normal form

23. In linear algebra, a _____ is a square matrix in which the entries outside the main diagonal are all zero. The diagonal entries themselves may or may not be zero. Thus, the matrix D = with n columns and n rows is diagonal if:

$$d_{i,j} = 0 \text{ if } i \neq j \qquad \forall i,j \in \{1, 2, \ldots, n\}$$

For example, the following matrix is diagonal:

$$\begin{bmatrix} 1 & 0 & 0 \\ 0 & 4 & 0 \\ 0 & 0 & -3 \end{bmatrix}.$$

The term _____ may sometimes refer to a rectangular _____, which is an m-by-n matrix with only the entries of the form $d_{i,i}$ possibly non-zero; for example,

$$\begin{bmatrix} 1 & 0 & 0 \\ 0 & 4 & 0 \\ 0 & 0 & -3 \\ 0 & 0 & 0 \end{bmatrix}, \text{ or } \begin{bmatrix} 1 & 0 & 0 & 0 & 0 \\ 0 & 4 & 0 & 0 & 0 \\ 0 & 0 & -3 & 0 & 0 \end{bmatrix}.$$

a. Design matrix
c. Transition matrix
b. Hankel matrix
d. Diagonal matrix

Chapter 6. Direct Methods for Solving Linear Systems

24. In mathematics, the term _____ has several different important meanings:

- An _____ is an equality that remains true regardless of the values of any variables that appear within it, to distinguish it from an equality which is true under more particular conditions. For this, the 'triple bar' symbol ≡ is sometimes used.
- In algebra, an _____ or _____ element of a set S with a binary operation Â· is an element e that, when combined with any element x of S, produces that same x. That is, eÂ·x = xÂ·e = x for all x in S.
    - The _____ function from a set S to itself, often denoted id or id_S, s the function such that i = x for all x in S. This function serves as the _____ element in the set of all functions from S to itself with respect to function composition.
    - In linear algebra, the _____ matrix of size n is the n-by-n square matrix with ones on the main diagonal and zeros elsewhere. This matrix serves as the _____ with respect to matrix multiplication.

A common example of the first meaning is the trigonometric _____

$$\sin^2 \theta + \cos^2 \theta = 1$$

which is true for all real values of θ, as opposed to

$$\cos \theta = 1,$$

which is true only for some values of θ, not all. For example, the latter equation is true when $\theta = 0$, false when $\theta = 2$

The concepts of 'additive _____' and 'multiplicative _____' are central to the Peano axioms. The number 0 is the 'additive _____' for integers, real numbers, and complex numbers. For the real numbers, for all $a \in \mathbb{R}$,

$$0 + a = a,$$

$$a + 0 = a, \text{ and}$$

$$0 + 0 = 0.$$

Similarly, The number 1 is the 'multiplicative _____' for integers, real numbers, and complex numbers.

a. Intersection
c. ARIA
b. Action
d. Identity

25. In linear algebra, the _____ or unit matrix of size n is the n-by-n square matrix with ones on the main diagonal and zeros elsewhere. It is denoted by I_n, or simply by I if the size is immaterial or can be trivially determined by the context. (In some fields, such as quantum mechanics, the _____ is denoted by a boldface one, 1; otherwise it is identical to I.)
   a. Unital
   b. Associativity
   c. Identity matrix
   d. Arity

26. In mathematics, a _____ is a system which is not linear. Less technically, a _____ is any problem where the variabl to be solved for cannot be written as a linear sum of independent components. A nonhomogenous system, which is linear apart from the presence of a function of the independent variables, is nonlinear according to a strict definition, but such systems are usually studied alongside linear systems, because they can be transformed to a linear system as long as a particular solution is known.
   a. George Dantzig
   b. Metric system
   c. Nonlinear system
   d. 1-center problem

27. A _____ number is a positive integer which has a positive divisor other than one or itself. By definition, every integer greater than one is either a prime number or a _____ number. zero and one are considered to be neither prime nor _____. For example, the integer 14 is a _____ number because it can be factored as 2 × 7.
   a. Composite
   b. Basis
   c. Discontinuity
   d. Key server

28. In mathematics, the _____ of a number n is the number that, when added to n, yields zero. The _____ of n is denoted −n. For example, 7 is −7, because 7 + (−7) = 0, and the _____ of −0.3 is 0.3, because −0.3 + 0.3 = 0.
   a. Arity
   b. Associativity
   c. Algebraic structure
   d. Additive inverse

29. If $A_1, A_2, ..., A_n$ are _____ square matrices over a field, then

$$(A_1 A_2 \cdots A_n)^{-1} = A_n^{-1} A_{n-1}^{-1} \cdots A_1^{-1}.$$

It becomes evident why this is the case if one attempts to find an inverse for the product of the A_is from first principles, that is, that we wish to determine B such that

$$(A_1 A_2 \cdots A_n) B = I$$

where B is the inverse matrix of the product. To remove A_1 from the product, we can then write

$$A_1^{-1}(A_1 A_2 \cdots A_n) B = A_1^{-1} I$$

which would reduce the equation to

$$(A_2 A_3 \cdots A_n) B = A_1^{-1} I.$$

Likewise, then, from

$$A_2^{-1}(A_2 A_3 \cdots A_n)B = A_2^{-1}A_1^{-1}I$$

which simplifies to

$$(A_3 A_4 \cdots A_n)B = A_2^{-1}A_1^{-1}I.$$

If one repeat the process up to A_n, the equation becomes

$$B = A_n^{-1}A_{n-1}^{-1} \cdots A_2^{-1}A_1^{-1}I$$

$$B = A_n^{-1}A_{n-1}^{-1} \cdots A_2^{-1}A_1^{-1}$$

but B is the inverse matrix, i.e. $B = (A_1 A_2 \cdots A_n)^{-1}$ so the property is established.

Over the field of real numbers, the set of singular n-by-n matrices, considered as a subset of $R^{n \times n}$, is a null set, i.e., has Lebesgue measure zero.

a. Nonsingular
c. Jordan normal form
b. Matrix pencil
d. Projection-valued measure

30. In mathematics, a _____ is an expression constructed from variables and constants, using the operations of addition, subtraction, multiplication, and constant non-negative whole number exponents. For example, $x^2 - 4x + 7$ is a _____, but $x^2 - 4/x + 7x^{3/2}$ is not, because its second term involves division by the variable x and also because its third term contains an exponent that is not a whole number.

_____s are one of the most important concepts in algebra and throughout mathematics and science.

a. Semifield
c. Coimage
b. Polynomial
d. Group extension

31. In mathematics, the idea of _____ has come to stand for a very general idea, extending the intuitive idea of 'gluing' in topology. Since the topologists' glue is actually the use of equivalence relations on topological spaces, the theory starts with some ideas on identification.

A sophisticated theory resulted.

a. Block size
c. Dominance
b. Deviance
d. Descent

32. In linear algebra, a _____ is a square matrix, A, that is equal to its transpose

$$A = A^T.$$

The entries of a _____ are symmetric with respect to the main diagonal. So if the entries are written as A =, then

$$a_{ij} = a_{ji}$$

for all indices i and j. The following 3×3 matrix is symmetric:

$$\begin{bmatrix} 1 & 2 & 3 \\ 2 & 4 & -5 \\ 3 & -5 & 6 \end{bmatrix}.$$

A matrix is called skew-symmetric or antisymmetric if its transpose is the same as its negative.

a. Symmetric matrix
c. Broken-line graph
b. Contour integration
d. Conway triangle notation

33. _____ generally conveys two primary meanings. The first is an imprecise sense of harmonious or aesthetically-pleasing proportionality and balance; such that it reflects beauty or perfection. The second meaning is a precise and well-defined concept of balance or 'patterned self-similarity' that can be demonstrated or proved according to the rules of a formal system: by geometry, through physics or otherwise.

a. Molecular symmetry
c. Tessellation
b. Symmetry
d. Symmetry breaking

34. In linear algebra, the _____ of a matrix A is another matrix A^T created by any one of the following equivalent actions:

- write the rows of A as the columns of A^T
- write the columns of A as the rows of A^T
- reflect A by its main diagonal to obtain A^T

Formally, the _____ of an m × n matrix A is the n × m matrix

$$A^T_{ij} = A_{ji} \text{ for } 1 \leq i \leq n, 1 \leq j \leq m.$$

- $\begin{bmatrix} 1 & 2 \\ 3 & 4 \end{bmatrix}^T = \begin{bmatrix} 1 & 3 \\ 2 & 4 \end{bmatrix}.$

- $\begin{bmatrix} 1 & 2 \\ 3 & 4 \\ 5 & 6 \end{bmatrix}^T = \begin{bmatrix} 1 & 3 & 5 \\ 2 & 4 & 6 \end{bmatrix}.$

For matrices A, B and scalar c we have the following properties of _____:

1. $\left(\mathbf{A}^T\right)^T = \mathbf{A}$

   Taking the _____ is an involution.

- $(\mathbf{A} + \mathbf{B})^T = \mathbf{A}^T + \mathbf{B}^T$

   The _____ respects addition.

- $(\mathbf{AB})^T = \mathbf{B}^T \mathbf{A}^T$

   Note that the order of the factors reverses. From this one can deduce that a square matrix A is invertible if and only if A^T is invertible, and in this case we have $^T = ^{-1}$. It is relatively easy to extend this result to the general case of multiple matrices, where we find that $^T = Z^T Y^T X^T ... C^T B^T A^T$.

- $(c\mathbf{A})^T = c\mathbf{A}^T$

   The _____ of a scalar is the same scalar. Together with, this states that the _____ is a linear map from the space of m × n matrices to the space of all n × m matrices.

- $\det(\mathbf{A}^T) = \det(\mathbf{A})$

Chapter 6. Direct Methods for Solving Linear Systems

The determinant of a matrix is the same as that of its _____.

- The dot product of two column vectors a and b can be computed as

$$\mathbf{a} \cdot \mathbf{b} = \mathbf{a}^T \mathbf{b},$$

which is written as $a_i\, b^i$ in Einstein notation.
- If A has only real entries, then $A^T A$ is a positive-semidefinite matrix.
- $(\mathbf{A}^T)^{-1} = (\mathbf{A}^{-1})^T$

The _____ of an invertible matrix is also invertible, and its inverse is the _____ of the inverse of the original matrix.

- If A is a square matrix, then its eigenvalues are equal to the eigenvalues of its _____.

A square matrix whose _____ is equal to itself is called a symmetric matrix; that is, A is symmetric if

$$\mathbf{A}^T = \mathbf{A}.$$

A square matrix whose _____ is also its inverse is called an orthogonal matrix; that is, G is orthogonal if

$$\mathbf{G}\mathbf{G}^T = \mathbf{G}^T\mathbf{G} = \mathbf{I}_n, \text{ the identity matrix.}$$

A square matrix whose _____ is equal to its negative is called skew-symmetric matrix; that is, A is skew-symmetric if

$$\mathbf{A}^T = -\mathbf{A}.$$

The conjugate _____ of the complex matrix A, written as A^*, is obtained by taking the _____ of A and the complex conjugate of each entry:

$$\mathbf{A}^* = (\overline{\mathbf{A}})^T = \overline{(\mathbf{A}^T)}.$$

If f: V→W is a linear map between vector spaces V and W with nondegenerate bilinear forms, we define the _____ of f to be the linear map ${}^t f$: W→V, determined by

$$B_V(v, {}^t f(w)) = B_W(f(v), w) \quad \forall\, v \in V, w \in W.$$

Here, B_V and B_W are the bilinear forms on V and W respectively. The matrix of the _____ of a map is the transposed matrix only if the bases are orthonormal with respect to their bilinear forms.

Over a complex vector space, one often works with sesquilinear forms instead of bilinear.

a. Cartan matrix
b. Polynomial matrix
c. Tridiagonal matrix
d. Transpose

35. In algebra, a _____ is a function depending on n that associates a scalar, de, to every n×n square matrix A. The fundamental geometric meaning of a _____ is as the scale factor for measure when A is regarded as a linear transformation. _____s are important both in calculus, where they enter the substitution rule for several variables, and in multilinear algebra.

a. Pfaffian
b. Functional determinant
c. 1-center problem
d. Determinant

36. In linear algebra, a _____ of a matrix A is the determinant of some smaller square matrix, cut down from A by removing one or more of its rows or columns.

_____s obtained by removing just one row and one column from square matrices are required for calculating matrix cofactors, which in turn are useful for computing both the determinant and inverse of square matrices.

Let A be an m × n matrix and k an integer with 0 < k ≤ m, and k ≤ n.

a. Homogeneity
b. Minor
c. Chiral
d. Block size

37. In mathematics, a _____ is a matrix formed by selecting certain rows and columns from a bigger matrix. That is, as an array, it is cut down to those entries constrained by row and column.

For example

$$\mathbf{A} = \begin{bmatrix} a_{11} & a_{12} & a_{13} & a_{14} \\ a_{21} & a_{22} & a_{23} & a_{24} \\ a_{31} & a_{32} & a_{33} & a_{34} \end{bmatrix}.$$

Then

$$\mathbf{A}[1, 2; 1, 3, 4] = \begin{bmatrix} a_{11} & a_{13} & a_{14} \\ a_{21} & a_{23} & a_{24} \end{bmatrix}$$

is a _____ of A formed by rows 1,2 and columns 1,3,4.

Chapter 6. Direct Methods for Solving Linear Systems

a. Matrix decomposition
c. Jordan matrix
b. Matrix unit
d. Submatrix

38. In the study of metric spaces in mathematics, there are various notions of two metrics on the same underlying space being 'the same', or _____.

In the following, M will denote a non-empty set and d_1 and d_2 will denote two metrics on M.

The two metrics d_1 and d_2 are said to be topologically _____ if they generate the same topology on M.

a. A posteriori
c. A chemical equation
b. A Mathematical Theory of Communication
d. Equivalent

39. In calculus, the _____ states that if a real-valued function f is continuous in the closed interval, then f must attain its maximum and minimum value, each at least once.

a. Average cost
c. Equity
b. Uncertainty quantification
d. Extreme Value Theorem

40. In mathematics, a _____ is a statement that can be proved on the basis of explicitly stated or previously agreed assumptions.

a. Logical value
c. Theorem
b. Boolean function
d. Disjunction introduction

41. In algebra, a _____ of an element in a quadratic extension field of a field K is its image under the unique non-identity automorphism of the extended field that fixes K. If the extension is generated by a square root of an element r of K, then the _____ of $a + b\sqrt{r}$ is $a - b\sqrt{r}$ for $a, b \in K$, and in particular in the case of the field C of complex numbers as an extension of the field R of real numbers, the complex _____ of a + bi is a − bi.

Forming the sum or product of any element of the extension field with its _____ always gives an element of K.

a. Relation algebra
c. Real structure
b. Conjugate
d. Trinomial

42. In vector calculus, the _____ of a scalar field is a vector field which points in the direction of the greatest rate of increase of the scalar field, and whose magnitude is the greatest rate of change.

A generalization of the _____ for functions on a Euclidean space which have values in another Euclidean space is the Jacobian. A further generalization for a function from one Banach space to another is the Fréchet derivative.

a. Stationary point
c. Gradient
b. Metric derivative
d. Directional derivative

Chapter 6. Direct Methods for Solving Linear Systems

43. In several fields of mathematics the term _____ is used with different but closely related meanings. They all relate to the notion of mapping the elements of a set to other elements of the same set, i.e., exchanging elements of a set.

The general concept of _____ can be defined more formally in different contexts:

In combinatorics, a _____ is usually understood to be a sequence containing each element from a finite set once, and only once.

a. Tensor product
c. Cyclic permutation

b. Linearly independent
d. Permutation

44. In mathematics, in matrix theory, a _____ is a square-matrix that has exactly one entry 1 in each row and each column and 0's elsewhere. Each such matrix represents a specific permutation of m elements and, when used to multiply another matrix, can produce that permutation in the rows or columns of the other matrix.

Given a permutation π of m elements,

$$\pi : \{1, \ldots, m\} \to \{1, \ldots, m\}$$

given in two-line form by

$$\begin{pmatrix} 1 & 2 & \cdots & m \\ \pi(1) & \pi(2) & \cdots & \pi(m) \end{pmatrix},$$

its _____ is the m × m matrix P_π whose entries are all 0 except that in row i, the entry equals 1.

a. Partitioned matrix
c. Hessenberg matrix

b. Permutation matrix
d. Cartan matrix

45. In mathematics, a matrix is said to be _____ if in every row of the matrix, the magnitude of the diagonal entry in that row is larger than the sum of the magnitudes of all the other (non-diagonal) entries in that row. More precisely, the matrix A is _____ if

<_____>½a_{ii}| > sum_{j eq i} |a_{ij}| quad ext{for all } i, ," src="http://upload.wikimedia.org/math/c/9/3/c93d69c3688c2b3d19ee8bb566427516.png"> _____>

where a_{ij} denotes the entry in the ith row and jth column.

The definition in the first paragraph sums entries across rows.

a. Successive over-relaxation
c. Stone's method

b. Power iteration
d. Diagonally dominant

Chapter 6. Direct Methods for Solving Linear Systems

46. In grammatical theory, definiteness is a feature of noun phrases, distinguishing between entities which are specific and identifiable in a given context (_____ noun phrases) and entities which are not (indefinite noun phrases Examples are:

- Free form: English the boy.
- Phrasal clitic: as in Basque: Cf. emakume ('woman'), emakume-a (woman-ART: 'the woman'), emakume ederr-a (woman beautiful-ART: 'the beautiful woman')
- Noun affix: as in Romanian: om ('man'), om-ul (man-ART: 'the man'); om-ul bun (man-ART good: 'the good man')
- Prefix on both noun and adjective: Arabic الكتاب الكبير (al-kitāb al-kabīr) with two instances of al- (DEF-book-DEF-big, literally, 'the book the big')

Germanic, Romance, Celtic, Semitic, and auxiliary languages generally have a _____ article, sometimes used as a postposition. Many other languages do not.

a. Sentence diagram
c. 1-center problem
b. Definite
d. Syntax

47. In mathematics, particularly matrix theory, a _____ is a sparse matrix, whose non-zero entries are confined to a diagonal band, comprising the main diagonal and zero or more diagonals on either side.

Formally, an n×n matrix A=($a_{i,j}$) is a _____ if all matrix elements are zero outside a diagonally bordered band whose range is determined by constants k_1 and k_2:

$$a_{i,j} = 0 \quad \text{if} \quad j < i - k_1 \quad \text{or} \quad j > i + k_2; \quad k_1, k_2 \geq 0.$$

The quantities k_1 and k_2 are the left and right half-bandwidth, respectively. The bandwidth of the matrix is $k_1 + k_2 + 1$ (in other words, the smallest number of adjacent diagonals to which the non-zero elements are confined.)

a. Band matrix
c. Vandermonde matrix
b. Hankel matrix
d. Positive-definite matrix

48. _____ is the difference between the upper and lower cutoff frequencies of, for example, a filter, a communication channel and is typically measured in hertz. In case of a baseband channel or signal, the _____ is equal to its upper cutoff frequency. _____ in hertz is a central concept in many fields, including electronics, information theory, radio communications, signal processing, and spectroscopy.

a. Critical point
c. Bandwidth
b. Completion
d. Lattice

49. In linear algebra, a _____ matrix is a matrix that is 'almost' a diagonal matrix. To be exact: a _____ matrix has nonzero elements only in the main diagonal, the first diagonal below this, and the first diagonal above the main diagonal.

For example, the following matrix is _____:

$$\begin{pmatrix} 1 & 4 & 0 & 0 \\ 3 & 4 & 1 & 0 \\ 0 & 2 & 3 & 4 \\ 0 & 0 & 1 & 3 \end{pmatrix}.$$

A determinant formed from a _____ matrix is known as a continuant.

a. Tridiagonal
c. Pascal matrix
b. Random matrix
d. Transition matrix

50. In linear algebra, a _____ is a matrix that is 'almost' a diagonal matrix. To be exact: a _____ has nonzero elements only in the main diagonal, the first diagonal below this, and the first diagonal above the main diagonal.

For example, the following matrix is tridiagonal:

$$\begin{pmatrix} 1 & 4 & 0 & 0 \\ 3 & 4 & 1 & 0 \\ 0 & 2 & 3 & 4 \\ 0 & 0 & 1 & 3 \end{pmatrix}$$

A determinant formed from a _____ is known as a continuant.

a. Stochastic matrix
c. Sylvester matrix
b. Transition matrix
d. Tridiagonal matrix

51. Augustin-Jean _____ (10 May 1788 - 14 July 1827), was a French physicist who contributed significantly to the establishment of the theory of wave optics. _____ studied the behaviour of light both theoretically and experimentally.

_____ was the son of an architect, born at Broglie (Eure.)

a. Kaisa Nyberg
c. Ralph C. Merkle
b. James Dickson Murray
d. Fresnel

52. _____, S(x) and C(x), are two transcendental functions named after Augustin-Jean Fresnel that are used in optics. They arise in the description of near field Fresnel diffraction phenomena, and are defined through the following integral representations:

$$S(x) = \int_0^x \sin(t^2)\, dt, \quad C(x) = \int_0^x \cos(t^2)\, dt.$$

The simultaneous parametric plot of S(x) and C(x) is the Cornu spiral, or clothoid.

Normalised _____, S(x) and C(x).
 a. Spiral
 b. Fresnel integrals
 c. Spiral of Theodorus
 d. Logarithmic spiral

Chapter 7. Iterative Methods for Solving Linear Systems

1. In mathematics, the _____ of a number n is the number that, when added to n, yields zero. The _____ of n is denoted −n. For example, 7 is −7, because 7 + (−7) = 0, and the _____ of −0.3 is 0.3, because −0.3 + 0.3 = 0.
   a. Associativity
   b. Arity
   c. Algebraic structure
   d. Additive inverse

2. In computational mathematics, an _____ attempts to solve a problem (for example an equation or system of equations) by finding successive approximations to the solution starting from an initial guess. This approach is in contrast to direct methods, which attempt to solve the problem by a finite sequence of operations, and, in the absence of rounding errors, would deliver an exact solution (like solving a linear system of equations Ax = b by Gaussian elimination.) _____s are usually the only choice for nonlinear equations.
   a. A chemical equation
   b. A posteriori
   c. A Mathematical Theory of Communication
   d. Iterative method

3. In mathematics, a _____ is a rectangular table of elements, which may be numbers or, more generally, any abstract quantities that can be added and multiplied. Matrices are used to describe linear equations, keep track of the coefficients of linear transformations and to record data that depend on multiple parameters. Matrices are described by the field of _____ theory.
   a. Compression
   b. Coherent
   c. Double counting
   d. Matrix

4. The _____ Evaluation and Review Technique, commonly abbreviated PERT, is a model for project management designed to analyze and represent the tasks involved in completing a given project.

   PERT is a method to analyze the involved tasks in completing a given project, especially the time needed to complete each task, and identifying the minimum time needed to complete the total project.

   This model was invented by Booz Allen Hamilton, Inc.

   a. Battle of the Sexes
   b. Program
   c. Key server
   d. Huge

5. In the mathematical subfield of numerical analysis a _____ is a matrix populated primarily with zeros.

   Conceptually, sparsity corresponds to systems which are loosely coupled. Consider a line of balls connected by springs from one to the next; this is a sparse system.

   a. Macdonald polynomials
   b. Pigeonhole principle
   c. Binomial coefficient
   d. Sparse matrix

6. In linear algebra, functional analysis and related areas of mathematics, a _____ is a function that assigns a strictly positive length or size to all vectors in a vector space, other than the zero vector. A seminorm, on the other hand, is allowed to assign zero length to some non-zero vectors.

   A simple example is the 2-dimensional Euclidean space R^2 equipped with the Euclidean _____.

a. Compression
c. Leibniz formula
b. Norm
d. Going up

7. In physics and in _____ calculus, a _____ is a concept characterized by a magnitude and a direction. A _____ can be thought of as an arrow in Euclidean space, drawn from an initial point A pointing to a terminal point B.
   a. Constraint
   b. Dominance
   c. Deviation
   d. Vector

8. In topology, the _____ of a subset S of a topological space X is the set of points which can be approached both from S and from the outside of S. More formally, it is the set of points in the closure of S, not belonging to the interior of S. An element of the _____ of S is called a _____ point of S.
   a. Bertrand paradox
   b. Boundary
   c. Heap
   d. Character

9. In mathematics, in the field of differential equations, a boundary value problem is a differential equation together with a set of additional restraints, called the _____. A solution to a boundary value problem is a solution to the differential equation which also satisfies the _____.

Boundary value problems arise in several branches of physics as any physical differential equation will have them.

   a. Boundary value problem
   b. Separation of variables
   c. Total differential equation
   d. Boundary conditions

10. In mathematics, an _____ is a statement about the relative size or order of two objects, or about whether they are the same or not

- The notation $a < b$ means that a is less than b.
- The notation $a > b$ means that a is greater than b.
- The notation $a \neq b$ means that a is not equal to b, but does not say that one is bigger than the other or even that they can be compared in size.

In all these cases, a is not equal to b, hence, '_____'.

These relations are known as strict _____

- The notation $a \leq b$ means that a is less than or equal to b;
- The notation $a \geq b$ means that a is greater than or equal to b;

An additional use of the notation is to show that one quantity is much greater than another, normally by several orders of magnitude.

- The notation $a \ll b$ means that a is much less than b.
- The notation $a \gg b$ means that a is much greater than b.

Chapter 7. Iterative Methods for Solving Linear Systems

If the sense of the _____ is the same for all values of the variables for which its members are defined, then the _____ is called an 'absolute' or 'unconditional' _____. If the sense of an _____ holds only for certain values of the variables involved, but is reversed or destroyed for other values of the variables, it is called a conditional _____.

An _____ may appear unsolvable because it only states whether a number is larger or smaller than another number; but it is possible to apply the same operations for equalities to inequalities. For example, to find x for the _____ 10x > 23 one would divide 23 by 10.

a. A Mathematical Theory of Communication
b. A posteriori
c. A chemical equation
d. Inequality

11. In mathematics, _____ is one of the basic operations defining a vector space in linear algebra. Note that _____ is different from scalar product which is an inner product between two vectors.

More specifically, if K is a field and V is a vector space over K, then _____ is a function from K × V to V.

a. Jordan normal form
b. Frobenius normal form
c. Non-negative matrix factorization
d. Scalar multiplication

12. In mathematics, the concept of a '_____' is used to describe the behavior of a function as its argument or input either 'gets close' to some point, or as the argument becomes arbitrarily large; or the behavior of a sequence's elements as their index increases indefinitely. _____s are used in calculus and other branches of mathematical analysis to define derivatives and continuity.

In formulas, _____ is usually abbreviated as lim.

a. Duality
b. Contact
c. Limit
d. Copula

13. As the positive integer n becomes larger and larger, the value n si becomes arbitrarily close to 1. We say that 'the limit of the sequence n si equals 1.'

The _____ is one of the oldest concepts in mathematical analysis. It provides a rigorous definition of the idea of a sequence converging towards a point called the limit.

a. Differential calculus
b. Limit of a sequence
c. Moment problem
d. Darboux function

14. In mathematics, a _____ is a system which is not linear. Less technically, a _____ is any problem where the variabl to be solved for cannot be written as a linear sum of independent components. A nonhomogenous system, which is linear apart from the presence of a function of the independent variables, is nonlinear according to a strict definition, but such systems are usually studied alongside linear systems, because they can be transformed to a linear system as long as a particular solution is known.

Chapter 7. Iterative Methods for Solving Linear Systems

    a. Metric system
    c. Nonlinear system
    b. George Dantzig
    d. 1-center problem

15. _____ is a finite element analysis (FEA) program that was originally developed for NASA in the late 1960s under United States government funding for the Aerospace industry. The MacNeal-Schwendler Corporation (MSC) was one of the principal and original developers of the public domain _____ code. _____ source code is integrated in a number of different software packages, which are distributed by a range of companies.
    a. SAMCEF
    c. Femap
    b. NASTRAN
    d. LS-DYNA

16. _____ is a branch of mathematics which focuses on the study of matrices. Initially a sub-branch of linear algebra, it has grown to cover subjects related to graph theory, algebra, combinatorics, and statistics as well.

The term matrix was first coined in 1848 by J.J. Sylvester as a name of an array of numbers.

    a. Semi-simple operators
    c. Pairing
    b. Segre classification
    d. Matrix theory

17. In mathematics, a _____ is a natural extension of the notion of a vector norm to matrices.

In what follows, K will denote the field of real or complex numbers. Consider the space $K^{m \times n}$ of all matrices with m rows and n columns with entries in K.

A _____ on $K^{m \times n}$ satisfies all the properties of vector norms.

    a. Matrix addition
    c. Pseudovector
    b. Nullspace
    d. Matrix norm

18. In mathematics, the _____ of a ring R, often denoted cha, is defined to be the smallest number of times one must add the ring's multiplicative identity element to itself to get the additive identity element; the ring is said to have _____ zero if this repeated sum never reaches the additive identity. That is, cha is the smallest positive number n such that

$$\underbrace{1 + \cdots + 1}_{n \text{ summands}} = 0$$

if such a number n exists, and 0 otherwise. The _____ may also be taken to be the exponent of the ring's additive group, that is, the smallest positive n such that

$$\underbrace{a + \cdots + a}_{n \text{ summands}} = 0$$

for every element a of the ring.

    a. Class
    c. Coherent
    b. Disk
    d. Characteristic

Chapter 7. Iterative Methods for Solving Linear Systems

19. In classical geometry, a _____ of a circle or sphere is any line segment from its center to its boundary. By extension, the _____ of a circle or sphere is the length of any such segment. The _____ is half the diameter. In science and engineering the term _____ of curvature is commonly used as a synonym for _____.

   a. Radius
   b. Duoprism
   c. Non-Euclidean geometry
   d. Birational geometry

20. In mathematics, a topological space X with topology Ω is said to be _____ if

   - 1) X is compact and T_0;
   - 2) The set C(X) of all relatively compact open subsets of (X,Ω) is a sublattice of Ω and a base for the topology.
   - 3) X is sober, that is any nonempty closed set F which is not a closure of a singleton {x} is a union of two closed sets which differ from F.

   a. Hedgehog space
   b. Cocountable topology
   c. Second-countable space
   d. Spectral

21. In mathematics, the _____ of a matrix or a bounded linear operator is the supremum among the absolute values of the elements in its spectrum, which is sometimes denoted by .

   Let $\lambda_1, \ldots, \lambda_s$ be the eigenvalues of a matrix $A \in \mathbb{C}^{n \times n}$. Then its _____ is defined as:

   $:= \max_i$

   The following lemma shows a simple yet useful upper bound for the _____ of a matrix:

   Lemma: Let $A \in \mathbb{C}^{n \times n}$ be a complex-valued matrix, its _____ and $||\hat{A}\cdot||$ a consistent matrix norm; then, for each $k \in \mathbb{N}$:

   $$\rho(A) \leq \|A^k\|^{1/k}, \forall k \in \mathbb{N}.$$

   Proof: Let be an eigenvector-eigenvalue pair for a matrix A.

   a. 120-cell
   b. 1-center problem
   c. Spectral theorem
   d. Spectral radius

22. In the absence of a more specific context, convergence denotes the approach toward a definite value, as time goes on; or to a definite point, a common view or opinion, or toward a fixed or equilibrium state. _____ is the adjectival form, and also a noun meaning an iterative approximation.

   In mathematics, convergence describes limiting behaviour, particularly of an infinite sequence or series, toward some limit.

a. Separable
b. Prime ideal theorem
c. Word problem
d. Convergent

23. In mathematics, the idea of _____ has come to stand for a very general idea, extending the intuitive idea of 'gluing' in topology. Since the topologists' glue is actually the use of equivalence relations on topological spaces, the theory starts with some ideas on identification.

A sophisticated theory resulted.

a. Dominance
b. Deviance
c. Descent
d. Block size

24. In linear algebra, _____ is an efficient algorithm for solving systems of linear equations, finding the rank of a matrix, and calculating the inverse of an invertible square matrix. _____ is named after German mathematician and scientist Carl Friedrich Gauss.

Elementary row operations are used to reduce a matrix to row echelon form.

a. Gaussian elimination
b. Cholesky decomposition
c. Conjugate gradient method
d. Crout matrix decomposition

25. In numerical mathematics, the _____ is a method for obtaining numerical approximations to the solutions of systems of equations, including certain types of elliptic partial differential equations, in particular Laplace's equation and its generalization, Poisson's equation. The function is assumed to be given on the boundary of a shape, and has to be computed on its interior.

This _____ should not be confused with the unrelated relaxation technique in mathematical optimization.

a. Strongly positive bilinear form
b. Primitive notion
c. Commutation matrix
d. Relaxation method

26. _____ (_____R) is a numerical method used to speed up convergence of the Gauss-Seidel method for solving a linear system of equations. A similar method can be used for any slowly converging iterative process. It was devised simultaneously by David M. Young and by H. Frankel in 1950 for the purpose of automatically solving linear systems on digital computers.

a. Successive over-relaxation
b. Portable, Extensible Toolkit for Scientific Computation
c. LU decomposition
d. Basic Linear Algebra Subprograms

68 Chapter 7. Iterative Methods for Solving Linear Systems

27. In grammatical theory, definiteness is a feature of noun phrases, distinguishing between entities which are specific and identifiable in a given context (_____ noun phrases) and entities which are not (indefinite noun phrases Examples are:

- Free form: English the boy.
- Phrasal clitic: as in Basque: Cf. emakume ('woman'), emakume-a (woman-ART: 'the woman'), emakume ederr-a (woman beautiful-ART: 'the beautiful woman')
- Noun affix: as in Romanian: om ('man'), om-ul (man-ART: 'the man'); om-ul bun (man-ART good: 'the good man')
- Prefix on both noun and adjective: Arabic الكتاب الكبير (al-kitāb al-kabīr) with two instances of al- (DEF-book-DEF-big, literally, 'the book the big')

Germanic, Romance, Celtic, Semitic, and auxiliary languages generally have a _____ article, sometimes used as a postposition. Many other languages do not.

a. 1-center problem
b. Sentence diagram
c. Syntax
d. Definite

28. A _____, sometimes denoted RW, is a mathematical formalization of a trajectory that consists of taking successive random steps. The results of _____ analysis have been applied to computer science, physics, ecology, economics and a number of other fields as a fundamental model for random processes in time. For example, the path traced by a molecule as it travels in a liquid or a gas, the search path of a foraging animal, the price of a fluctuating stock and the financial status of a gambler can all be modeled as _____s.

a. Random walk
b. Bose-Einstein statistics
c. Phase transition
d. Vector spaces

29. Walking is the main form of animal locomotion on land, distinguished from running and crawling. When carried out in shallow waters, it is usually described as wading and when performed over a steeply rising object or an obstacle it becomes scrambling or climbing. The word _____ is descended from the Old English wealcan 'to roll'.

a. Walk
b. 1-center problem
c. 2-3 heap
d. 120-cell

30. A _____ is a structure built to span a gorge, valley, road, railroad track, river, body of water for the purpose of providing passage over the obstacle. Designs of _____s will vary depending on the function of the _____ and the nature of the terrain where the _____ is to be constructed. Roman _____ of Córdoba, Spain, built in the 1st century BC. Ponte di Pietra in Verona, Italy. A log _____ in the French Alps near Vallorcine. An English 18th century example of a _____ in the Palladian style, with shops on the span: Pulteney _____, Bath A Han Dynasty Chinese miniature model of two residential towers joined by a _____

The first _____s were made by nature -- as simple as a log fallen across a stream.

a. 120-cell
b. Bridge
c. 1-center problem
d. 2-3 heap

31. The Institute of Electrical and Electronics Engineers or _____ (read eye-triple-e) is an international non-profit, professional organization for the advancement of technology related to electricity. It has the most members of any technical professional organization in the world, with more than 365,000 members in around 150 countries.

Chapter 7. Iterative Methods for Solving Linear Systems

The _____ is incorporated in the State of New York, United States.

a. IEEE
c. A posteriori

b. A Mathematical Theory of Communication
d. A chemical equation

32. In mathematics, a _____ is a statement that can be proved on the basis of explicitly stated or previously agreed assumptions.

a. Boolean function
c. Theorem

b. Disjunction introduction
d. Logical value

33. In mathematical analysis, the _____ states that every continuous function defined on an interval [a,b] can be uniformly approximated as closely as desired by a polynomial function. Because polynomials are the simplest functions, and computers can directly evaluate polynomials, this theorem has both practical and theoretical relevance, especially in polynomial interpolation. The original version of this result was established by Karl Weierstrass in 1885.

a. Weierstrass Approximation Theorem
c. Space-filling curve

b. Peano curve
d. Tietze extension theorem

34. In numerical analysis, the _____ associated with a problem is a measure of that problem's amenability to digital computation, that is, how numerically well-conditioned the problem is. A problem with a low _____ is said to be well-conditioned, while a problem with a high _____ is said to be ill-conditioned.

For example, the _____ associated with the linear equation Ax = b gives a bound on how inaccurate the solution x will be after approximate solution.

a. Condition number
c. Numerical continuation

b. Dynamic relaxation
d. Meshfree methods

35. In linear algebra, a _____ is a matrix with the unit fraction elements

$$H_{ij} = \frac{1}{i+j-1}.$$

For example, this is the 5 × 5 _____:

$$H = \begin{bmatrix} 1 & \frac{1}{2} & \frac{1}{3} & \frac{1}{4} & \frac{1}{5} \\ \frac{1}{2} & \frac{1}{3} & \frac{1}{4} & \frac{1}{5} & \frac{1}{6} \\ \frac{1}{3} & \frac{1}{4} & \frac{1}{5} & \frac{1}{6} & \frac{1}{7} \\ \frac{1}{4} & \frac{1}{5} & \frac{1}{6} & \frac{1}{7} & \frac{1}{8} \\ \frac{1}{5} & \frac{1}{6} & \frac{1}{7} & \frac{1}{8} & \frac{1}{9} \end{bmatrix}.$$

The _____ can be regarded as derived from the integral

$$H_{ij} = \int_0^1 x^{i+j-2}\, dx,$$

that is, as a Gramian matrix for powers of x. It is a Hankel matrix.

The Hilbert matrices are canonical examples of ill-conditioned matrices, making them notoriously difficult to use in numerical computation.

a. Triangular matrix
b. Generalized minimal residual method
c. Hilbert matrix
d. Symbolic Cholesky decomposition

36. In mathematics, an _____ is a vector space with the additional structure of inner product. This additional structure associates each pair of vectors in the space with a scalar quantity known as the inner product of the vectors. Inner products allow the rigorous introduction of intuitive geometrical notions such as the length of a vector or the angle between two vectors.
a. A chemical equation
b. A posteriori
c. A Mathematical Theory of Communication
d. Inner product space

37. In algebra, a _____ of an element in a quadratic extension field of a field K is its image under the unique non-identity automorphism of the extended field that fixes K. If the extension is generated by a square root of an element r of K, then the _____ of $a + b\sqrt{r}$ is $a - b\sqrt{r}$ for $a, b \in K$, and in particular in the case of the field C of complex numbers as an extension of the field R of real numbers, the complex _____ of a + bi is a − bi.

Forming the sum or product of any element of the extension field with its _____ always gives an element of K.

a. Conjugate
b. Relation algebra
c. Real structure
d. Trinomial

38. In mathematics, the _____ is an algorithm for the numerical solution of particular systems of linear equations, namely those whose matrix is symmetric and positive definite. The _____ is an iterative method, so it can be applied to sparse systems which are too large to be handled by direct methods such as the Cholesky decomposition. Such systems arise regularly when numerically solving partial differential equations.
a. Symbolic Cholesky decomposition
b. Circulant matrix
c. Power iteration
d. Conjugate gradient method

39. In vector calculus, the _____ of a scalar field is a vector field which points in the direction of the greatest rate of increase of the scalar field, and whose magnitude is the greatest rate of change.

A generalization of the _____ for functions on a Euclidean space which have values in another Euclidean space is the Jacobian. A further generalization for a function from one Banach space to another is the Fréchet derivative.

Chapter 7. Iterative Methods for Solving Linear Systems

a. Stationary point
c. Gradient
b. Metric derivative
d. Directional derivative

40. In commutative algebra, the notions of an element _____ over a ring, and of an _____ extension of rings, are a generalization of the notions in field theory of an element being algebraic over a field, and of an algebraic extension of fields.

The special case of greatest interest in number theory is that of complex numbers _____ over the ring of integers Z.

The term ring will be understood to mean commutative ring with a unit.

a. Integral
c. Antidifferentiation
b. Integral test for convergence
d. Arc length

41. In statistics, _____ has two related meanings:

- the arithmetic _____.
- the expected value of a random variable, which is also called the population _____.

It is sometimes stated that the '_____' _____s average. This is incorrect if '_____' is taken in the specific sense of 'arithmetic _____' as there are different types of averages: the _____, median, and mode. For instance, average house prices almost always use the median value for the average.

For a real-valued random variable X, the _____ is the expectation of X.

a. Probability
c. Statistical population
b. Proportional hazards model
d. Mean

42. In calculus, the _____ states, roughly, that given a section of a smooth curve, there is at least one point on that section at which the derivative of the curve is equal to the 'average' derivative of the section. It is used to prove theorems that make global conclusions about a function on an interval starting from local hypotheses about derivatives at points of the interval.

This theorem can be understood concretely by applying it to motion: if a car travels one hundred miles in one hour, so that its average speed during that time was 100 miles per hour, then at some time its instantaneous speed must have been exactly 100 miles per hour.

a. Fundamental Theorem of Calculus
c. Functional integration
b. Calculus controversy
d. Mean Value Theorem

43. In mathematics, the _____ or saddle-point approximation is a method used to approximate integrals of the form

$$\int_a^b e^{Mf(x)}\,dx$$

Chapter 7. Iterative Methods for Solving Linear Systems

where fs method, which in fact concerns the special case of real-valued functions f admitting a maximum at a real point.

Assume that the function f0.

a. Master theorem
b. Riemann-Lebesgue lemma
c. 1-center problem
d. Steepest descent method

Chapter 8. Approximation Theory

1. In mathematics, _____ is concerned with how functions can best be approximated with simpler functions, and with quantitatively characterizing the errors introduced thereby. Note that what is meant by best and simpler will depend on the application.

A closely related topic is the approximation of functions by generalized Fourier series, that is, approximations based upon summation of a series of terms based upon orthogonal polynomials.

a. Approximation theory
b. A chemical equation
c. A Mathematical Theory of Communication
d. A posteriori

2. In topology, the _____ of a subset S of a topological space X is the set of points which can be approached both from S and from the outside of S. More formally, it is the set of points in the closure of S, not belonging to the interior of S. An element of the _____ of S is called a _____ point of S.

a. Heap
b. Bertrand paradox
c. Character
d. Boundary

3. In mathematics, in the field of differential equations, a boundary value problem is a differential equation together with a set of additional restraints, called the _____. A solution to a boundary value problem is a solution to the differential equation which also satisfies the _____.

Boundary value problems arise in several branches of physics as any physical differential equation will have them.

a. Boundary value problem
b. Total differential equation
c. Separation of variables
d. Boundary conditions

4. The method of _____ or ordinary _____ is used to solve overdetermined systems. _____ is often applied in statistical contexts, particularly regression analysis.

_____ can be interpreted as a method of fitting data.

a. Non-linear least squares
b. System equivalence
c. Rata Die
d. Least squares

5. The _____ Evaluation and Review Technique, commonly abbreviated PERT, is a model for project management designed to analyze and represent the tasks involved in completing a given project.

PERT is a method to analyze the involved tasks in completing a given project, especially the time needed to complete each task, and identifying the minimum time needed to complete the total project.

This model was invented by Booz Allen Hamilton, Inc.

a. Battle of the Sexes
b. Huge
c. Key server
d. Program

Chapter 8. Approximation Theory

6. The word _____ has many distinct meanings in different fields of knowledge, depending on their methodologies and the context of discussion. Broadly speaking we can say that a _____ is some kind of belief or claim that (supposedly) explains, asserts, or consolidates some class of claims. Additionally, in contrast with a theorem the statement of the _____ is generally accepted only in some tentative fashion as opposed to regarding it as having been conclusively established.
   a. Transport of structure
   b. Defined
   c. Per mil
   d. Theory

7. In statistics, the _____ of an element of a data set is the absolute difference between that element and a given point. Typically the point from which the deviation is measured is the value of either the median or the mean of the data set.

$$|D| = |x_i - m|$$

where

   $|D|$ is the _____,
   x_i is the data element
   and m is the chosen measure of central tendency of the data set--sometimes the mean, but most often the median.

   a. A chemical equation
   b. A Mathematical Theory of Communication
   c. Interquartile range
   d. Absolute deviation

8. In mathematics and statistics, _____ is a measure of difference for interval and ratio variables between the observed value and the mean. The sign of _____, either positive or negative, indicates whether the observation is larger than or smaller than the mean. The magnitude of the value reports how different an observation is from the mean.
   a. Filter
   b. Conchoid
   c. Deviation
   d. Functional

9. In statistical decision theory, where we are faced with the problem of estimating a deterministic parameter $\theta \in \Theta$ from observations $x \in \mathcal{X}$. An estimator δ^M is called _____ if it's maximal risk is minimal among all estimators of θ. In a sense this means that δ^M is an estimator which performs best in the worst possible case allowed in the problem.
   a. Gittins index
   b. Championship mobilization
   c. Regret
   d. Minimax

10. In mathematics, specifically in combinatorial commutative algebra, a convex lattice polytope P is called _____ if it has the following property: given any positive integer n, every lattice point of the dilation nP, obtained from P by scaling its vertices by the factor n and taking the convex hull of the resulting points, can be written as the sum of exactly n lattice points in P. This property plays an important role in the theory of toric varieties, where it corresponds to projective normality of the toric variety determined by P.

The simplex in R^k with the vertices at the origin and along the unit coordinate vectors is _____.

a. Polytetrahedron
b. Demihypercubes
c. Hypercube
d. Normal

11. A justification for choosing this criterion is given in properties below. This minimization problem has a unique solution, provided that the n columns of the matrix X are linearly independent, given by solving the _____

$$(X^\top X)\hat{\boldsymbol{\beta}} = X^\top \mathbf{y}.$$

The primary application of linear least squares is in data fitting. Given a set of m data points $y_1, y_2, \ldots, y_m$, consisting of experimentally measured values taken at m values $x_1, x_2, \ldots, x_m$ of an independent variable (x_i may be scalar or vector quantities), and given a model function $y = f(x, \boldsymbol{\beta})$, with $\boldsymbol{\beta} = (\beta_1, \beta_2, \ldots, \beta_n)$, it is desired to find the parameters β_j such that the model function fits 'best' the data.

a. Slack variable
b. Shekel function
c. Constraint optimization
d. Normal equations

12. _____ was the Allied codename for any of several German teleprinter stream ciphers used during World War II. Enciphered teleprinter traffic was used between German High Command and Army Group commanders in the field, so its intelligence value was of the highest strategic value to the Allies. This traffic normally passed over landlines, but as German forces extended their reach out of western Europe, they had to resort to wireless transmission.

a. Fish
b. Colossus
c. Function
d. Divide and conquer

13. In signal processing, _____ is the reduction of a continuous signal to a discrete signal. A common example is the conversion of a sound wave to a sequence of samples.

A sample refers to a value or set of values at a point in time and/or space.

a. Decidable
b. Sampling
c. Disk
d. Converse logic

14. In statistics, the _____ or _____ function is the partial derivative, with respect to some parameter θ, of the logarithm of the likelihood function. If the observation is X and its likelihood is L, then the _____ V can be found through the chain rule:

$$V = \frac{\partial}{\partial \theta} \log L(\theta; X) = \frac{1}{L(\theta; X)} \frac{\partial L(\theta; X)}{\partial \theta}.$$

Note that V is a function of θ and the observation X, so that, in general, it is not a statistic. Note also that V indicates the sensitivity of L.

a. Functional
b. Cleaver
c. Score
d. Deviation

Chapter 8. Approximation Theory

15. In probability theory, a probability distribution is called _____ if its cumulative distribution function is _____. That is equivalent to saying that for random variables X with the distribution in question, Pr[X = a] = 0 for all real numbers a. If the distribution of X is _____ then X is called a _____ random variable.
   a. Concatenated codes
   b. Continuous phase modulation
   c. Continuous
   d. Conull set

16. In linear algebra, a _____ is a matrix with the unit fraction elements

$$H_{ij} = \frac{1}{i+j-1}.$$

For example, this is the 5 × 5 _____:

$$H = \begin{bmatrix} 1 & \frac{1}{2} & \frac{1}{3} & \frac{1}{4} & \frac{1}{5} \\ \frac{1}{2} & \frac{1}{3} & \frac{1}{4} & \frac{1}{5} & \frac{1}{6} \\ \frac{1}{3} & \frac{1}{4} & \frac{1}{5} & \frac{1}{6} & \frac{1}{7} \\ \frac{1}{4} & \frac{1}{5} & \frac{1}{6} & \frac{1}{7} & \frac{1}{8} \\ \frac{1}{5} & \frac{1}{6} & \frac{1}{7} & \frac{1}{8} & \frac{1}{9} \end{bmatrix}.$$

The _____ can be regarded as derived from the integral

$$H_{ij} = \int_0^1 x^{i+j-2}\, dx,$$

that is, as a Gramian matrix for powers of x. It is a Hankel matrix.

The Hilbert matrices are canonical examples of ill-conditioned matrices, making them notoriously difficult to use in numerical computation.

   a. Triangular matrix
   b. Hilbert matrix
   c. Generalized minimal residual method
   d. Symbolic Cholesky decomposition

17. In mathematics, a _____ is a rectangular table of elements, which may be numbers or, more generally, any abstract quantities that can be added and multiplied. Matrices are used to describe linear equations, keep track of the coefficients of linear transformations and to record data that depend on multiple parameters. Matrices are described by the field of _____ theory.
   a. Compression
   b. Double counting
   c. Matrix
   d. Coherent

Chapter 8. Approximation Theory

18. The mathematical concept of a _____ expresses the intuitive idea of deterministic dependence between two quantities, one of which is viewed as primary and the other as secondary. A _____ then is a way to associate a unique output for each input of a specified type, for example, a real number or an element of a given set.
   a. Function
   b. Coherent
   c. Going up
   d. Grill

19. In linear algebra, a family of vectors is linearly independent if none of them can be written as a linear combination of finitely many other vectors in the collection. A family of vectors which is not linearly independent is called _____. For instance, in the three-dimensional real vector space R^3 we have the following example.
   a. Normal extension
   b. Restriction of scalars
   c. Coimage
   d. Linearly dependent

20. In mathematics, a _____ is a statement that can be proved on the basis of explicitly stated or previously agreed assumptions.
   a. Disjunction introduction
   b. Theorem
   c. Boolean function
   d. Logical value

21. In mathematical analysis, the _____ states that every continuous function defined on an interval [a,b] can be uniformly approximated as closely as desired by a polynomial function. Because polynomials are the simplest functions, and computers can directly evaluate polynomials, this theorem has both practical and theoretical relevance, especially in polynomial interpolation. The original version of this result was established by Karl Weierstrass in 1885.
   a. Peano curve
   b. Tietze extension theorem
   c. Space-filling curve
   d. Weierstrass Approximation Theorem

22. In the physical sciences, _____ is a measurement of the gravitational force acting on an object. Near the surface of the Earth, the acceleration due to gravity is approximately constant; this means that an object's _____ is roughly proportional to its mass.

In commerce and in many other applications, _____ means the same as mass as that term is used in physics.

   a. 2-3 heap
   b. 120-cell
   c. 1-center problem
   d. Weight

23. A _____ is a mathematical device used when performing a sum, integral, or average in order to give some elements more of a 'weight' than others. They occur frequently in statistics and analysis, and are closely related to the concept of a measure. _____s can be constructed in both discrete and continuous settings.
   a. Mountain pass theorem
   b. Ramp function
   c. Weight function
   d. Kantorovich inequality

24. In linear algebra, _____ is an efficient algorithm for solving systems of linear equations, finding the rank of a matrix, and calculating the inverse of an invertible square matrix. _____ is named after German mathematician and scientist Carl Friedrich Gauss.

Elementary row operations are used to reduce a matrix to row echelon form.

a. Gaussian elimination
c. Crout matrix decomposition
b. Conjugate gradient method
d. Cholesky decomposition

25. In mathematics, two vectors are _____ if they are perpendicular. For example, a subway and the street above, although they do not physically intersect, are _____ if they cross at a right angle.
   a. Additive identity
   b. Unique factorization domain
   c. Orthogonal
   d. Algebraic structure

26. In linear algebra, two vectors in an inner product space are _____ if they are orthogonal and both of unit length. A set of vectors form an _____ set if all vectors in the set are mutually orthogonal and all of unit length. An _____ set which forms a basis is called an _____ basis.
   a. Orthogonal Procrustes problem
   b. Orthogonalization
   c. Orthogonal complement
   d. Orthonormal

27. In mathematics, particularly linear algebra and numerical analysis, the _____ is a method for orthogonalizing a set of vectors in an inner product space, most commonly the Euclidean space R^n. The _____ takes a finite, linearly independent set S = {v_1, ââ,¬¦, v_n} and generates an orthogonal set S' = {u_1, ââ,¬¦, u_n} that spans the same subspace as S.

The method is named for J>ørgen Pedersen Gram and Erhard Schmidt but it appeared earlier in the work of Laplace and Cauchy.

   a. Dot product
   b. Homogeneous coordinates
   c. Gram-Schmidt process
   d. Linear algebra

28. In mathematics, a _____ is an expression constructed from variables and constants, using the operations of addition, subtraction, multiplication, and constant non-negative whole number exponents. For example, $x^2 - 4x + 7$ is a _____, but $x^2 - 4/x + 7x^{3/2}$ is not, because its second term involves division by the variable x and also because its third term contains an exponent that is not a whole number.

_____s are one of the most important concepts in algebra and throughout mathematics and science.

   a. Polynomial
   b. Group extension
   c. Semifield
   d. Coimage

29. In mathematics, the _____ of a ring R, often denoted cha, is defined to be the smallest number of times one must add the ring's multiplicative identity element to itself to get the additive identity element; the ring is said to have _____ zero if this repeated sum never reaches the additive identity. That is, cha is the smallest positive number n such that

$$\underbrace{1 + \cdots + 1}_{n \text{ summands}} = 0$$

if such a number n exists, and 0 otherwise. The _____ may also be taken to be the exponent of the ring's additive group, that is, the smallest positive n such that

$$\underbrace{a + \cdots + a}_{n \text{ summands}} = 0$$

for every element a of the ring.

a. Disk
b. Coherent
c. Characteristic
d. Class

30. In mathematics, given a linear transformation, an _____ of that linear transformation is a nonzero vector which, when that transformation is applied to it, may change in length, but not direction.

For each _____ of a linear transformation, there is a corresponding scalar value called an eigenvalue for that vector, which determines the amount the _____ is scaled under the linear transformation. For example, an eigenvalue of +2 means that the _____ is doubled in length and points in the same direction.

a. Angular momentum
b. Ensemble
c. Eigenvector
d. Uncertainty principle

31. In physics and in _____ calculus, a _____ is a concept characterized by a magnitude and a direction. A _____ can be thought of as an arrow in Euclidean space, drawn from an initial point A pointing to a terminal point B.

a. Deviation
b. Dominance
c. Constraint
d. Vector

32. In mathematics the _____, named after Pafnuty Chebyshev, are a sequence of orthogonal polynomials which are related to de Moivre's formula and which are easily defined recursively, like Fibonacci or Lucas numbers. One usually distinguishes between _____ of the first kind which are denoted T_n and _____ of the second kind which are denoted U_n. The letter T is used because of the alternative transliterations of the name Chebyshev as Tchebyshef or Tschebyscheff.

a. Chebyshev polynomials
b. Boubaker polynomial
c. Quadratic function
d. Padovan polynomials

33. The need for _____s arises in many branches of applied mathematics, and computer science in particular. In general, a _____ problem asks us to select a function among a well-defined class that closely matches a target function in a task-specific way.

One can distinguish two major classes of _____ problems: First, for known target functions approximation theory is the branch of numerical analysis that investigates how certain known functions can be approximated by a specific class of functions that often have desirable properties.

a. P-Laplacian
b. Berezin transform
c. Walsh functions
d. Function approximation

34. In mathematics, a _____ is any function which can be written as the ratio of two polynomial functions. _____ of degree 2 :

$$y = \frac{x^2 - 3x - 2}{x^2 - 4}$$

In the case of one variable, x, a _____ is a function of the form

$$f(x) = \frac{P(x)}{Q(x)}$$

where P and Q are polynomial function in x and Q is not the zero polynomial. The domain of f is the set of all points x for which the denominator Q

a. Legendre rational functions
b. 1-center problem
c. 120-cell
d. Rational function

35. In mathematics, a _____ is often represented as the sum of a sequence of terms. That is, a _____ is represented as a list of numbers with addition operations between them, for example this arithmetic sequence:

1 + 2 + 3 + 4 + 5 + ... + 99 + 100

In most cases of interest the terms of the sequence are produced according to a certain rule, such as by a formula, by an algorithm, by a sequence of measurements, or even by a random number generator.

a. Concavity
b. Contact
c. Blind
d. Series

36. The _____, named for John Tukey, is a single-step multiple comparison procedure which applies simultaneously to the set of all pairwise comparisons

$\mu_i - \mu_j$

The confidence coefficient for the set, when all sample sizes are equal, is exactly $1 - \alpha$. For unequal sample sizes, the confidence coefficient is greater than $1 - \alpha$. In other words, the _____ is conservative when there are unequal sample sizes.

a. Convergence of random variables
b. CIE 1931 XYZ color space
c. Continuous-time Markov process
d. Tukey method

Chapter 8. Approximation Theory

37. A _____ number is a positive integer which has a positive divisor other than one or itself. By definition, every integer greater than one is either a prime number or a _____ number.zero and one are considered to be neither prime nor _____. For example, the integer 14 is a _____ number because it can be factored as 2 × 7.
    a. Basis
    b. Key server
    c. Discontinuity
    d. Composite

38. The _____ of an angle is the ratio of the length of the opposite side to the length of the hypotenuse. In our case

$$\sin A = \frac{\text{opposite}}{\text{hypotenuse}} = \frac{a}{h}.$$

Note that this ratio does not depend on size of the particular right triangle chosen, as long as it contains the angle A, since all such triangles are similar.

The cosine of an angle is the ratio of the length of the adjacent side to the length of the hypotenuse.

   a. Sine
   b. Right angle
   c. Law of sines
   d. Trigonometric functions

39. In mathematics, the _____ functions are functions of an angle; they are important when studying triangles and modeling periodic phenomena, among many other applications.
    a. Gudermannian function
    b. Trigonometric
    c. Coversine
    d. Law of sines

40. In mathematics, a _____ decomposes a periodic function into a sum of simple oscillating functions, namely sines and cosines. The study of _____ is a branch of Fourier analysis. _____ were introduced by Joseph Fourier for the purpose of solving the heat equation in a metal plate.
    a. Triangle wave
    b. 1-center problem
    c. Fourier series of a periodic function converges
    d. Fourier series

41. A _____ is an efficient algorithm to compute the discrete Fourier transform and its inverse

A DFT decomposes a sequence of values into components of different frequencies.

   a. 1-center problem
   b. 120-cell
   c. 2-3 heap
   d. Fast Fourier transform

42. In mathematics and in the sciences, a _____ (plural: _____e, formulæ or _____s) is a concise way of expressing information symbolically (as in a mathematical or chemical _____), or a general relationship between quantities. One of many famous _____e is Albert Einstein's E = mc² (see special relativity

In mathematics, a _____ is a key to solve an equation with variables. For example, the problem of determining the volume of a sphere is one that requires a significant amount of integral calculus to solve.

a. 120-cell
c. 2-3 heap
b. 1-center problem
d. Formula

Chapter 9. Approximating Eigenvalues

1. In mathematics, given a linear transformation, an _____ of that linear transformation is a nonzero vector which, when that transformation is applied to it, may change in length, but not direction.

For each _____ of a linear transformation, there is a corresponding scalar value called an eigenvalue for that vector, which determines the amount the _____ is scaled under the linear transformation. For example, an eigenvalue of +2 means that the _____ is doubled in length and points in the same direction.

   a. Uncertainty principle
   b. Eigenvector
   c. Ensemble
   d. Angular momentum

2. In linear algebra, a family of vectors is linearly independent if none of them can be written as a linear combination of finitely many other vectors in the collection. A family of vectors which is not linearly independent is called _____. For instance, in the three-dimensional real vector space R^3 we have the following example.
   a. Normal extension
   b. Restriction of scalars
   c. Coimage
   d. Linearly dependent

3. In linear algebra, a family of vectors is _____ if none of them can be written as a linear combination of finitely many other vectors in the collection. A family of vectors which is not _____ is called linearly dependent. For instance, in the three-dimensional real vector space R^3 we have the following example.
   a. Direct product
   b. Linear combinations
   c. Binary function
   d. Linearly independent

4. The _____ Evaluation and Review Technique, commonly abbreviated PERT, is a model for project management designed to analyze and represent the tasks involved in completing a given project.

PERT is a method to analyze the involved tasks in completing a given project, especially the time needed to complete each task, and identifying the minimum time needed to complete the total project.

This model was invented by Booz Allen Hamilton, Inc.

   a. Battle of the Sexes
   b. Key server
   c. Program
   d. Huge

5. In physics and in _____ calculus, a _____ is a concept characterized by a magnitude and a direction. A _____ can be thought of as an arrow in Euclidean space, drawn from an initial point A pointing to a terminal point B.
   a. Dominance
   b. Vector
   c. Constraint
   d. Deviation

6. In mathematics, _____ is one of the basic operations defining a vector space in linear algebra. Note that _____ is different from scalar product which is an inner product between two vectors.

More specifically, if K is a field and V is a vector space over K, then _____ is a function from K × V to V.

   a. Non-negative matrix factorization
   b. Frobenius normal form
   c. Jordan normal form
   d. Scalar multiplication

7. In linear algebra, _____ is an efficient algorithm for solving systems of linear equations, finding the rank of a matrix, and calculating the inverse of an invertible square matrix. _____ is named after German mathematician and scientist Carl Friedrich Gauss.

Elementary row operations are used to reduce a matrix to row echelon form.

a. Cholesky decomposition
b. Conjugate gradient method
c. Crout matrix decomposition
d. Gaussian elimination

8. _____ is the self-government of a nation, country or some portion thereof, generally exercising sovereignty.

The term _____ is used in contrast to subjugation, which refers to a region as a 'territory' --subject to the political and military control of an external government. The word is sometimes used in a weaker sense to contrast with hegemony, the indirect control of one nation by another, more powerful nation.

a. A Mathematical Theory of Communication
b. A chemical equation
c. A posteriori
d. Independence

9. In mathematics, a _____ is a rectangular table of elements, which may be numbers or, more generally, any abstract quantities that can be added and multiplied. Matrices are used to describe linear equations, keep track of the coefficients of linear transformations and to record data that depend on multiple parameters. Matrices are described by the field of _____ theory.

a. Compression
b. Coherent
c. Double counting
d. Matrix

10. In mathematics, two vectors are _____ if they are perpendicular. For example, a subway and the street above, although they do not physically intersect, are _____ if they cross at a right angle.

a. Algebraic structure
b. Additive identity
c. Unique factorization domain
d. Orthogonal

11. In matrix theory, a real _____ is a square matrix Q whose transpose is its inverse:

$$Q^T Q = Q Q^T = I.$$

A special _____ is an _____ with determinant +1:

$$\det Q = +1.$$

An _____ is the real specialization of a unitary matrix, and thus always a normal matrix. Although we consider only real matrices here, the definition can be used for matrices with entries from any field. However, orthogonal matrices arise naturally from inner products, and for matrices of complex numbers that leads instead to the unitary requirement.

Chapter 9. Approximating Eigenvalues

    a. Orthogonal matrix
    b. Unitary matrix
    c. Unimodular polynomial matrix
    d. Alternating sign matrix

12.   In linear algebra, two vectors in an inner product space are _____ if they are orthogonal and both of unit length. A set of vectors form an _____ set if all vectors in the set are mutually orthogonal and all of unit length. An _____ set which forms a basis is called an _____ basis.
    a. Orthogonal complement
    b. Orthogonalization
    c. Orthogonal Procrustes problem
    d. Orthonormal

13.   In the case of Gaussian elimination, it is best to choose a pivot element with large absolute value. This improves the numerical stability. In _____, the algorithm considers all entries in the column of the matrix that is currently being considered, picks the entry with largest absolute value, and finally swaps rows such that this entry is the pivot in question.
    a. 2-3 heap
    b. 120-cell
    c. 1-center problem
    d. Partial Pivoting

14.   In mathematics, a _____ is a statement that can be proved on the basis of explicitly stated or previously agreed assumptions.
    a. Boolean function
    b. Theorem
    c. Logical value
    d. Disjunction introduction

15.   In mathematics and in the sciences, a _____ (plural: _____e, formulæ or _____s) is a concise way of expressing information symbolically (as in a mathematical or chemical _____), or a general relationship between quantities. One of many famous _____e is Albert Einstein's E = mc^2 (see special relativity

In mathematics, a _____ is a key to solve an equation with variables. For example, the problem of determining the volume of a sphere is one that requires a significant amount of integral calculus to solve.

    a. 2-3 heap
    b. 120-cell
    c. 1-center problem
    d. Formula

16.   _____ is a branch of mathematics which focuses on the study of matrices. Initially a sub-branch of linear algebra, it has grown to cover subjects related to graph theory, algebra, combinatorics, and statistics as well.

The term matrix was first coined in 1848 by J.J. Sylvester as a name of an array of numbers.

    a. Matrix theory
    b. Semi-simple operators
    c. Pairing
    d. Segre classification

17.   In linear algebra, two n-by-n matrices A and B over the field K are called _____ if there exists an invertible n-by-n matrix P over K such that

$$P^{-1}AP = B.$$

One of the meanings of the term similarity transformation is such a transformation of a matrix A into a matrix B.

Similarity is an equivalence relation on the space of square matrices.

_____ matrices share many properties:

- rank
- determinant
- trace
- eigenvalues
- characteristic polynomial
- minimal polynomial
- elementary divisors

There are two reasons for these facts:

- two _____ matrices can be thought of as describing the same linear map, but with respect to different bases
- the map $X \mapsto P^{-1}XP$ is an automorphism of the associative algebra of all n-by-n matrices, as the one-object case of the above category of all matrices.

Because of this, for a given matrix A, one is interested in finding a simple 'normal form' B which is _____ to A -- the study of A then reduces to the study of the simpler matrix B.

a. Blinding
c. Coherence
b. Dense
d. Similar

18. In linear algebra, two n-by-n matrices A and B over the field K are called similar if there exists an invertible n-by-n matrix P over K such that

$$P^{-1}AP = B.$$

One of the meanings of the term _____ is such a transformation of a matrix A into a matrix B.

Similarity is an equivalence relation on the space of square matrices.

Chapter 9. Approximating Eigenvalues

Similar matrices share many properties:

- rank
- determinant
- trace
- eigenvalues
- characteristic polynomial
- minimal polynomial
- elementary divisors

There are two reasons for these facts:

- two similar matrices can be thought of as describing the same linear map, but with respect to different bases
- the map $X \mapsto P^{-1}XP$ is an automorphism of the associative algebra of all n-by-n matrices, as the one-object case of the above category of all matrices.

Because of this, for a given matrix A, one is interested in finding a simple 'normal form' B which is similar to A -- the study of A then reduces to the study of the simpler matrix B.

a. Transpose
c. Hadamard matrix

b. Cartan matrix
d. Similarity transformation

19. A _____ is a simple shape of Euclidean geometry consisting of those points in a plane which are at a constant distance, called the radius, from a fixed point, called the center. A _____ with center A is sometimes denoted by the symbol A.

A chord of a _____ is a line segment whose two endpoints lie on the _____.

a. Circular segment
c. Circumcircle

b. Malfatti circles
d. Circle

20. In mathematics, the _____s are an extension of the real numbers obtained by adjoining an imaginary unit, denoted i, which satisfies:

$$i^2 = -1.$$

Every _____ can be written in the form a + bi, where a and b are real numbers called the real part and the imaginary part of the _____, respectively.

_____s are a field, and thus have addition, subtraction, multiplication, and division operations. These operations extend the corresponding operations on real numbers, although with a number of additional elegant and useful properties, e.g., negative real numbers can be obtained by squaring _____s.

Chapter 9. Approximating Eigenvalues

a. Complex number
c. Real part
b. 120-cell
d. 1-center problem

21. In grammatical theory, definiteness is a feature of noun phrases, distinguishing between entities which are specific and identifiable in a given context (_____ noun phrases) and entities which are not (indefinite noun phrases Examples are:

- Free form: English the boy.
- Phrasal clitic: as in Basque: Cf. emakume ('woman'), emakume-a (woman-ART: 'the woman'), emakume ederr-a (woman beautiful-ART: 'the beautiful woman')
- Noun affix: as in Romanian: om ('man'), om-ul (man-ART: 'the man'); om-ul bun (man-ART good: 'the good man')
- Prefix on both noun and adjective: Arabic الكتاب الكبير (al-kitāb al-kabīr) with two instances of al- (DEF-book-DEF-big, literally, 'the book the big')

Germanic, Romance, Celtic, Semitic, and auxiliary languages generally have a _____ article, sometimes used as a postposition. Many other languages do not.

a. Sentence diagram
c. 1-center problem
b. Definite
d. Syntax

22. Augustin-Jean _____ (10 May 1788 - 14 July 1827), was a French physicist who contributed significantly to the establishment of the theory of wave optics. _____ studied the behaviour of light both theoretically and experimentally.

_____ was the son of an architect, born at Broglie (Eure.)

a. Fresnel
c. James Dickson Murray
b. Ralph C. Merkle
d. Kaisa Nyberg

23. _____, S(x) and C(x), are two transcendental functions named after Augustin-Jean Fresnel that are used in optics. They arise in the description of near field Fresnel diffraction phenomena, and are defined through the following integral representations:

$$S(x) = \int_0^x \sin(t^2)\, dt, \quad C(x) = \int_0^x \cos(t^2)\, dt.$$

The simultaneous parametric plot of S(x) and C(x) is the Cornu spiral, or clothoid.

Normalised _____, S(x) and C(x).
a. Spiral
c. Spiral of Theodorus
b. Logarithmic spiral
d. Fresnel integrals

24. In commutative algebra, the notions of an element _____ over a ring, and of an _____ extension of rings, are a generalization of the notions in field theory of an element being algebraic over a field, and of an algebraic extension of fields.

Chapter 9. Approximating Eigenvalues 89

The special case of greatest interest in number theory is that of complex numbers _____ over the ring of integers Z.

The term ring will be understood to mean commutative ring with a unit.

a. Antidifferentiation
c. Integral test for convergence
b. Integral
d. Arc length

25. In mathematics, the idea of _____ has come to stand for a very general idea, extending the intuitive idea of 'gluing' in topology. Since the topologists' glue is actually the use of equivalence relations on topological spaces, the theory starts with some ideas on identification.

A sophisticated theory resulted.

a. Block size
c. Deviance
b. Descent
d. Dominance

26. In mathematics, a _____ is an expression constructed from variables and constants, using the operations of addition, subtraction, multiplication, and constant non-negative whole number exponents. For example, $x^2 - 4x + 7$ is a _____, but $x^2 - 4/x + 7x^{3/2}$ is not, because its second term involves division by the variable x and also because its third term contains an exponent that is not a whole number.

_____s are one of the most important concepts in algebra and throughout mathematics and science.

a. Group extension
c. Coimage
b. Semifield
d. Polynomial

27. In mathematics, the _____ of a number n is the number that, when added to n, yields zero. The _____ of n is denoted −n. For example, 7 is −7, because 7 + (−7) = 0, and the _____ of −0.3 is 0.3, because −0.3 + 0.3 = 0.

a. Associativity
c. Algebraic structure
b. Arity
d. Additive inverse

28. In applied mathematics and mechanical engineering, the _____ is a widely used, classical method for the calculation of the natural vibration frequency of a structure in the second or higher order. It is a direct variational method in which the minimum of a functional defined on a normed linear space is approximated by a linear combination of elements from that space. This method will yield solutions when an analytical form for the true solution may be intractable.

a. 2-3 heap
c. 1-center problem
b. 120-cell
d. Rayleigh-Ritz method

29. The _____ concept is a mathematical formalization for any fixed "rule" which describes the time dependence of a point's position in its ambient space. The concept unifies very different types of such "rules" in mathematics: the different choices made for how time is measured and the special properties the ambient space may give an idea of the vastity of the class of objects described by this concept.

a. Dynamical system
c. 1-center problem
b. Metric system
d. George Dantzig

30. In linear algebra, a _____ matrix is a matrix that is 'almost' a diagonal matrix. To be exact: a _____ matrix has nonzero elements only in the main diagonal, the first diagonal below this, and the first diagonal above the main diagonal.

For example, the following matrix is _____:

$$\begin{pmatrix} 1 & 4 & 0 & 0 \\ 3 & 4 & 1 & 0 \\ 0 & 2 & 3 & 4 \\ 0 & 0 & 1 & 3 \end{pmatrix}.$$

A determinant formed from a _____ matrix is known as a continuant.

a. Pascal matrix
c. Random matrix
b. Transition matrix
d. Tridiagonal

31. A _____ is a movement of an object in a circular motion. A two-dimensional object rotates around a center of _____. A three-dimensional object rotates around a line called an axis.

a. Steiner-Lehmus theorem
c. Square lattice
b. Homothetic center
d. Rotation

32. In linear algebra, a _____ is a square matrix, A, that is equal to its transpose

$$A = A^T.$$

The entries of a _____ are symmetric with respect to the main diagonal. So if the entries are written as A =, then

$$a_{ij} = a_{ji}$$

for all indices i and j. The following 3×3 matrix is symmetric:

$$\begin{bmatrix} 1 & 2 & 3 \\ 2 & 4 & -5 \\ 3 & -5 & 6 \end{bmatrix}.$$

A matrix is called skew-symmetric or antisymmetric if its transpose is the same as its negative.

a. Contour integration
c. Broken-line graph
b. Conway triangle notation
d. Symmetric matrix

Chapter 10. Solutions of Systems of Nonlinear Equations

1. In mathematics, a _____ is a system which is not linear. Less technically, a _____ is any problem where the variabl to be solved for cannot be written as a linear sum of independent components. A nonhomogenous system, which is linear apart from the presence of a function of the independent variables, is nonlinear according to a strict definition, but such systems are usually studied alongside linear systems, because they can be transformed to a linear system as long as a particular solution is known.

   a. Metric system
   b. 1-center problem
   c. George Dantzig
   d. Nonlinear system

2. The _____ Evaluation and Review Technique, commonly abbreviated PERT, is a model for project management designed to analyze and represent the tasks involved in completing a given project.

   PERT is a method to analyze the involved tasks in completing a given project, especially the time needed to complete each task, and identifying the minimum time needed to complete the total project.

   This model was invented by Booz Allen Hamilton, Inc.

   a. Huge
   b. Key server
   c. Program
   d. Battle of the Sexes

3. The _____, named for John Tukey, is a single-step multiple comparison procedure which applies simultaneously to the set of all pairwise comparisons

   $\mu_i - \mu_j$

   The confidence coefficient for the set, when all sample sizes are equal, is exactly $1 - \alpha$. For unequal sample sizes, the confidence coefficient is greater than $1 - \alpha$. In other words, the _____ is conservative when there are unequal sample sizes.

   a. CIE 1931 XYZ color space
   b. Tukey method
   c. Continuous-time Markov process
   d. Convergence of random variables

4. The mathematical concept of a _____ expresses the intuitive idea of deterministic dependence between two quantities, one of which is viewed as primary and the other as secondary. A _____ then is a way to associate a unique output for each input of a specified type, for example, a real number or an element of a given set.

   a. Going up
   b. Grill
   c. Coherent
   d. Function

5. In probability theory, a probability distribution is called _____ if its cumulative distribution function is _____. That is equivalent to saying that for random variables X with the distribution in question, $Pr[X = a] = 0$ for all real numbers a. If the distribution of X is _____ then X is called a _____ random variable.

   a. Concatenated codes
   b. Continuous phase modulation
   c. Conull set
   d. Continuous

6. In mathematics, the concept of a '_____' is used to describe the behavior of a function as its argument or input either 'gets close' to some point, or as the argument becomes arbitrarily large; or the behavior of a sequence's elements as their index increases indefinitely. _____s are used in calculus and other branches of mathematical analysis to define derivatives and continuity.

Chapter 10. Solutions of Systems of Nonlinear Equations

In formulas, _____ is usually abbreviated as lim.

a. Duality
c. Copula

b. Limit
d. Contact

7. In vector calculus, the _____ is shorthand for either the _____ matrix or its determinant, the _____ determinant.

In algebraic geometry the _____ of a curve means the _____ variety: a group variety associated to the curve, in which the curve can be embedded.

These concepts are all named after the mathematician Carl Gustav Jacob Jacobi.

a. Jacobian
c. Shift theorem

b. Surface integral
d. Monkey saddle

8. In mathematics, a _____ is a rectangular table of elements, which may be numbers or, more generally, any abstract quantities that can be added and multiplied. Matrices are used to describe linear equations, keep track of the coefficients of linear transformations and to record data that depend on multiple parameters. Matrices are described by the field of _____ theory.

a. Coherent
c. Double counting

b. Matrix
d. Compression

9. In applied mathematics and mechanical engineering, the _____ is a widely used, classical method for the calculation of the natural vibration frequency of a structure in the second or higher order. It is a direct variational method in which the minimum of a functional defined on a normed linear space is approximated by a linear combination of elements from that space. This method will yield solutions when an analytical form for the true solution may be intractable.

a. 120-cell
c. 2-3 heap

b. Rayleigh-Ritz method
d. 1-center problem

10. In mathematics, the idea of _____ has come to stand for a very general idea, extending the intuitive idea of 'gluing' in topology. Since the topologists' glue is actually the use of equivalence relations on topological spaces, the theory starts with some ideas on identification.

A sophisticated theory resulted.

a. Deviance
c. Descent

b. Block size
d. Dominance

Chapter 10. Solutions of Systems of Nonlinear Equations

11. _____ is a term in mathematics. It can refer to:

   - a _____ line, in geometry
   - the trigonometric function called _____
   - the _____ method, a root-finding algorithm in numerical analysis

   a. Large set
   c. Solvable
   b. Separable
   d. Secant

12. In mathematics and in the sciences, a _____ (plural: _____e, formulæ or _____s) is a concise way of expressing information symbolically (as in a mathematical or chemical _____), or a general relationship between quantities. One of many famous _____e is Albert Einstein's E = mc^2 (see special relativity

   In mathematics, a _____ is a key to solve an equation with variables. For example, the problem of determining the volume of a sphere is one that requires a significant amount of integral calculus to solve.

   a. 1-center problem
   c. 2-3 heap
   b. 120-cell
   d. Formula

13. In mathematics, the _____ or saddle-point approximation is a method used to approximate integrals of the form

$$\int_a^b e^{Mf(x)}\,dx$$

   where fs method, which in fact concerns the special case of real-valued functions f admitting a maximum at a real point.

   Assume that the function f0.

   a. Master theorem
   c. Riemann-Lebesgue lemma
   b. 1-center problem
   d. Steepest descent method

14. A _____ is a simple shape of Euclidean geometry consisting of those points in a plane which are at a constant distance, called the radius, from a fixed point, called the center. A _____ with center A is sometimes denoted by the symbol A.

   A chord of a _____ is a line segment whose two endpoints lie on the _____.

   a. Malfatti circles
   c. Circumcircle
   b. Circular segment
   d. Circle

15. The multiple integral is a type of definite integral extended to functions of more than one real variable, for example, fz = x^2 + y^2. The rectangular region at the bottom of the body is the domain of integration, while the surface is the graph of the two-variable function to be integrated.

Chapter 10. Solutions of Systems of Nonlinear Equations

Introduction

Just as the definite integral of a positive function of one variable represents the area of the region between the graph of the function and the x-axis, the _____ of a positive function of two variables represents the volume of the region between the surface defined by the function and the plane which contains its domain.

   a. Risch algorithm   b. Double Integral
   c. Solid of revolution   d. Signed measure

16. In commutative algebra, the notions of an element _____ over a ring, and of an _____ extension of rings, are a generalization of the notions in field theory of an element being algebraic over a field, and of an algebraic extension of fields.

The special case of greatest interest in number theory is that of complex numbers _____ over the ring of integers Z.

The term ring will be understood to mean commutative ring with a unit.

   a. Integral test for convergence   b. Arc length
   c. Antidifferentiation   d. Integral

17. In mathematics, a _____ is a statement that can be proved on the basis of explicitly stated or previously agreed assumptions.
   a. Disjunction introduction   b. Boolean function
   c. Logical value   d. Theorem

18. _____ is a fundamental construction of differential calculus and admits many possible generalizations within the fields of mathematical analysis, combinatorics, algebra, and geometry.

In real, complex, and functional analysis, _____s are generalized to functions of several real or complex variables and functions between topological vector spaces. An important case is the variational _____ in the calculus of variations.

   a. Derivative   b. Metric derivative
   c. Lin-Tsien equation   d. Functional derivative

19. In mathematics, the _____ of a multivariate differentiable function along a given vector V at a given point P intuitively represents the instantaneous rate of change of the function, moving through P, in the direction of V. It therefore generalizes the notion of a partial derivative, in which the direction is always taken parallel to one of the coordinate axes.

The _____ is a special case of the Gâteaux derivative.

a. Directional derivative
c. Gradient
b. Metric derivative
d. Second derivative test

20. In vector calculus, the _____ of a scalar field is a vector field which points in the direction of the greatest rate of increase of the scalar field, and whose magnitude is the greatest rate of change.

A generalization of the _____ for functions on a Euclidean space which have values in another Euclidean space is the Jacobian. A further generalization for a function from one Banach space to another is the Fréchet derivative.

a. Metric derivative
c. Directional derivative
b. Gradient
d. Stationary point

Chapter 11. Boundary-Value Problems for Ordinary Differential Equations

1. The multiple integral is a type of definite integral extended to functions of more than one real variable, for example, fz = x^2 + y^2. The rectangular region at the bottom of the body is the domain of integration, while the surface is the graph of the two-variable function to be integrated.

Introduction

Just as the definite integral of a positive function of one variable represents the area of the region between the graph of the function and the x-axis, the _____ of a positive function of two variables represents the volume of the region between the surface defined by the function and the plane which contains its domain.

a. Double Integral
c. Risch algorithm
b. Solid of revolution
d. Signed measure

2. In commutative algebra, the notions of an element _____ over a ring, and of an _____ extension of rings, are a generalization of the notions in field theory of an element being algebraic over a field, and of an algebraic extension of fields.

The special case of greatest interest in number theory is that of complex numbers _____ over the ring of integers Z.

The term ring will be understood to mean commutative ring with a unit.

a. Antidifferentiation
c. Integral test for convergence
b. Arc length
d. Integral

3. Suppose that φ : M → N is a smooth map between smooth manifolds; then the _____ of φ at a point x is, in some sense, the best linear approximation of φ near x. It can be viewed as generalization of the total derivative of ordinary calculus. Explicitly, it is a linear map from the tangent space of M at x to the tangent space of N at φ
a. Grill
c. Boundary
b. Concurrent
d. Differential

4. _____s arise in many problems in physics, engineering, etc. The following examples show how to solve _____s in a few simple cases when an exact solution exists.

A separable linear ordinary _____ of the first order has the general form:

$$\frac{dy}{dt} + f(t)y = 0$$

where f is some known function.

a. Nullcline
c. Nahm equations
b. Differential equation
d. Homogeneous differential equation

5. The _____ Evaluation and Review Technique, commonly abbreviated PERT, is a model for project management designed to analyze and represent the tasks involved in completing a given project.

98   *Chapter 11. Boundary-Value Problems for Ordinary Differential Equations*

PERT is a method to analyze the involved tasks in completing a given project, especially the time needed to complete each task, and identifying the minimum time needed to complete the total project.

This model was invented by Booz Allen Hamilton, Inc.

   a. Battle of the Sexes   b. Program
   c. Key server   d. Huge

6.   In topology, the _____ of a subset S of a topological space X is the set of points which can be approached both from S and from the outside of S. More formally, it is the set of points in the closure of S, not belonging to the interior of S. An element of the _____ of S is called a _____ point of S.

   a. Character   b. Bertrand paradox
   c. Heap   d. Boundary

7.   In mathematics, in the field of differential equations, a _____ is a differential equation together with a set of additional restraints, called the boundary conditions. A solution to a _____ is a solution to the differential equation which also satisfies the boundary conditions.

_____s arise in several branches of physics as any physical differential equation will have them.

   a. Separation of variables   b. Normal mode
   c. Riccati equation   d. Boundary value problem

8.   In mathematics and in the sciences, a _____ (plural: _____e, formulæ or _____s) is a concise way of expressing information symbolically (as in a mathematical or chemical _____), or a general relationship between quantities. One of many famous _____e is Albert Einstein's E = mc^2 (see special relativity

In mathematics, a _____ is a key to solve an equation with variables. For example, the problem of determining the volume of a sphere is one that requires a significant amount of integral calculus to solve.

   a. 120-cell   b. 1-center problem
   c. 2-3 heap   d. Formula

9.   A _____ is an algebraic equation in which each term is either a constant or the product of a constant and a single variable. _____s can have one, two, three or more variables.

_____s occur with great regularity in applied mathematics.

   a. Linear equation   b. Quartic equation
   c. Difference of two squares   d. Quadratic equation

10.   In numerical analysis, the _____ is a method for solving a boundary value problem by reducing it to the solution of an initial value problem. The following exposition may be clarified by this illustration of the _____.

For a boundary value problem of a second-order ordinary differential equation, the method is stated as follows.

Chapter 11. Boundary-Value Problems for Ordinary Differential Equations

a. Verlet integration
c. Symplectic integrator
b. Midpoint method
d. Shooting method

11. In applied mathematics and mechanical engineering, the _____ is a widely used, classical method for the calculation of the natural vibration frequency of a structure in the second or higher order. It is a direct variational method in which the minimum of a functional defined on a normed linear space is approximated by a linear combination of elements from that space. This method will yield solutions when an analytical form for the true solution may be intractable.
a. 1-center problem
c. 2-3 heap
b. 120-cell
d. Rayleigh-Ritz method

12.

- _____ difference
- _____ energy

a. 120-cell
c. 1-center problem
b. 2-3 heap
d. Potential

13. In numerical analysis, _____ is a sequence acceleration method, used to improve the rate of convergence of a sequence. It is named after Lewis Fry Richardson, who introduced the technique in the early 20th century. In the words of Birkhoff and Rota, '...
a. Constructions of low-discrepancy sequences
c. Cascade algorithm
b. Truncation error
d. Richardson extrapolation

14. In the mathematical subfield of numerical analysis, a _____ is a spline function that has minimal support with respect to a given degree, smoothness, and domain partition. A fundamental theorem states that every spline function of a given degree, smoothness, and domain partition, can be represented as a linear combination of _____s of that same degree and smoothness, and over that same partition. The term _____ was coined by Isaac Jacob Schoenberg and is short for basis spline.
a. Non-uniform rational B-spline
c. Cubic Hermite spline
b. 1-center problem
d. B-spline

15. In mathematics, a _____ is a system which is not linear. Less technically, a _____ is any problem where the variabl to be solved for cannot be written as a linear sum of independent components. A nonhomogenous system, which is linear apart from the presence of a function of the independent variables, is nonlinear according to a strict definition, but such systems are usually studied alongside linear systems, because they can be transformed to a linear system as long as a particular solution is known.
a. Metric system
c. 1-center problem
b. Nonlinear system
d. George Dantzig

16. In mathematics, a _____ is a statement that can be proved on the basis of explicitly stated or previously agreed assumptions.
a. Boolean function
c. Disjunction introduction
b. Theorem
d. Logical value

Chapter 11. Boundary-Value Problems for Ordinary Differential Equations

17. A _____ is a mathematical expression of the form f- f- a, one gets a difference quotient. The approximation of derivatives by _____s plays a central role in _____ methods for the numerical solution of differential equations, especially boundary value problems.

   a. Finite-difference methods
   b. 1-center problem
   c. Discrete Poisson equation
   d. Finite Difference

18. In algebra, a _____ of an element in a quadratic extension field of a field K is its image under the unique non-identity automorphism of the extended field that fixes K. If the extension is generated by a square root of an element r of K, then the _____ of $a + b\sqrt{r}$ is $a - b\sqrt{r}$ for $a, b \in K$, and in particular in the case of the field C of complex numbers as an extension of the field R of real numbers, the complex _____ of a + bi is a − bi.

   Forming the sum or product of any element of the extension field with its _____ always gives an element of K.

   a. Trinomial
   b. Conjugate
   c. Relation algebra
   d. Real structure

19. In vector calculus, the _____ of a scalar field is a vector field which points in the direction of the greatest rate of increase of the scalar field, and whose magnitude is the greatest rate of change.

   A generalization of the _____ for functions on a Euclidean space which have values in another Euclidean space is the Jacobian. A further generalization for a function from one Banach space to another is the Fréchet derivative.

   a. Directional derivative
   b. Stationary point
   c. Gradient
   d. Metric derivative

20. In linear algebra, a _____ is a set of vectors that, in a linear combination, can represent every vector in a given vector space or free module, and such that no element of the set can be represented as a linear combination of the others. In other words, a _____ is a linearly independent spanning set. This picture illustrates the standard _____ in R^2.

   a. Dot plot
   b. Conchoid
   c. Chiral
   d. Basis

21. In mathematics, particularly numerical analysis, a _____ is an element of the basis for a function space. The term is a degeneration of the term basis vector for a more general vector space; that is, each function in the function space can be represented as a linear combination of the _____s.

   The collection of quadratic polynomials with real coefficients has {1, t, t^2} as a basis.

   a. Constructions of low-discrepancy sequences
   b. Meshfree methods
   c. Basis function
   d. Bernstein polynomial

22. The mathematical concept of a _____ expresses the intuitive idea of deterministic dependence between two quantities, one of which is viewed as primary and the other as secondary. A _____ then is a way to associate a unique output for each input of a specified type, for example, a real number or an element of a given set.

Chapter 11. Boundary-Value Problems for Ordinary Differential Equations

a. Function
b. Coherent
c. Going up
d. Grill

23. In mathematics, specifically in combinatorial commutative algebra, a convex lattice polytope P is called _____ if it has the following property: given any positive integer n, every lattice point of the dilation nP, obtained from P by scaling its vertices by the factor n and taking the convex hull of the resulting points, can be written as the sum of exactly n lattice points in P. This property plays an important role in the theory of toric varieties, where it corresponds to projective normality of the toric variety determined by P.

The simplex in R^k with the vertices at the origin and along the unit coordinate vectors is _____.

a. Demihypercubes
b. Hypercube
c. Polytetrahedron
d. Normal

24. A justification for choosing this criterion is given in properties below. This minimization problem has a unique solution, provided that the n columns of the matrix X are linearly independent, given by solving the _____

$$(X^\top X)\hat{\boldsymbol{\beta}} = X^\top \mathbf{y}.$$

The primary application of linear least squares is in data fitting. Given a set of m data points $y_1, y_2, \ldots, y_m$, consisting of experimentally measured values taken at m values $x_1, x_2, \ldots, x_m$ of an independent variable (x_i may be scalar or vector quantities), and given a model function $y = f(x, \boldsymbol{\beta})$, with $\boldsymbol{\beta} = (\beta_1, \beta_2, \ldots, \beta_n)$, it is desired to find the parameters β_j such that the model function fits 'best' the data.

a. Shekel function
b. Constraint optimization
c. Slack variable
d. Normal equations

25. _____ is a method of constructing new data points from a discrete set of known data points.

a. Interpolation
b. Integration by substitution
c. Archimedes' use of infinitesimals
d. Uniform convergence

Chapter 12. Numerical Methods for Partial-Differential Equations

1. The multiple integral is a type of definite integral extended to functions of more than one real variable, for example, fz = x^2 + y^2. The rectangular region at the bottom of the body is the domain of integration, while the surface is the graph of the two-variable function to be integrated.

Introduction

Just as the definite integral of a positive function of one variable represents the area of the region between the graph of the function and the x-axis, the _____ of a positive function of two variables represents the volume of the region between the surface defined by the function and the plane which contains its domain.

   a. Solid of revolution
   b. Double Integral
   c. Risch algorithm
   d. Signed measure

2. In commutative algebra, the notions of an element _____ over a ring, and of an _____ extension of rings, are a generalization of the notions in field theory of an element being algebraic over a field, and of an algebraic extension of fields.

The special case of greatest interest in number theory is that of complex numbers _____ over the ring of integers Z.

The term ring will be understood to mean commutative ring with a unit.

   a. Integral test for convergence
   b. Arc length
   c. Antidifferentiation
   d. Integral

3. The _____ Evaluation and Review Technique, commonly abbreviated PERT, is a model for project management designed to analyze and represent the tasks involved in completing a given project.

PERT is a method to analyze the involved tasks in completing a given project, especially the time needed to complete each task, and identifying the minimum time needed to complete the total project.

This model was invented by Booz Allen Hamilton, Inc.

   a. Program
   b. Huge
   c. Battle of the Sexes
   d. Key server

4. In topology, the _____ of a subset S of a topological space X is the set of points which can be approached both from S and from the outside of S. More formally, it is the set of points in the closure of S, not belonging to the interior of S. An element of the _____ of S is called a _____ point of S.
   a. Heap
   b. Character
   c. Boundary
   d. Bertrand paradox

5. In mathematics, in the field of differential equations, a boundary value problem is a differential equation together with a set of additional restraints, called the _____. A solution to a boundary value problem is a solution to the differential equation which also satisfies the _____.

Chapter 12. Numerical Methods for Partial-Differential Equations

Boundary value problems arise in several branches of physics as any physical differential equation will have them.

a. Total differential equation
b. Boundary value problem
c. Separation of variables
d. Boundary conditions

6. Suppose that φ : M → N is a smooth map between smooth manifolds; then the _____ of φ at a point x is, in some sense, the best linear approximation of φ near x. It can be viewed as generalization of the total derivative of ordinary calculus. Explicitly, it is a linear map from the tangent space of M at x to the tangent space of N at φ

a. Concurrent
b. Boundary
c. Grill
d. Differential

7. _____s arise in many problems in physics, engineering, etc. The following examples show how to solve _____s in a few simple cases when an exact solution exists.

A separable linear ordinary _____ of the first order has the general form:

$$\frac{dy}{dt} + f(t)y = 0$$

where f is some known function.

a. Nahm equations
b. Homogeneous differential equation
c. Nullcline
d. Differential equation

8. In differential geometry, a discipline within mathematics, a _____ is a subset of the tangent bundle of a manifold satisfying certain properties. _____s are used to build up notions of integrability, and specifically of a foliation of a manifold

a. Discontinuity
b. Distribution
c. Coherence
d. Constraint

9. The _____ is a partial differential equation which describes density fluctuations in a material undergoing diffusion. It is also used to describe processes exhibiting diffusive-like behaviour, for instance the 'diffusion' of alleles in a population in population genetics.

The equation is usually written as:

$$\frac{\partial \phi(\vec{r}, t)}{\partial t} = \nabla \cdot \left(D(\phi, \vec{r}) \nabla \phi(\vec{r}, t) \right),$$

where $\phi(\vec{r}, t)$ is the density of the diffusing material at location $\vec{r}$ and time t and $D(\phi, \vec{r})$ is the collective diffusion coefficient for density φ at location $\vec{r}$; the nabla symbol ∇ represents the vector differential operator del acting on the space coordinates.

a. 120-cell
b. 2-3 heap
c. 1-center problem
d. Diffusion equation

10. A vibration in a string is a wave. Usually a _____ produces a sound whose frequency in most cases is constant. Therefore, since frequency characterizes the pitch, the sound produced is a constant note.

a. Harmonic oscillator
b. Vibrating string
c. 1-center problem
d. 120-cell

11. The _____ , is achieved in a packed stadium when successive groups of spectators briefly stand and raise their arms. Each spectator is required to rise at the same time as those straight in front and behind, and slightly after the person immediately to either the right or the left. Immediately upon stretching to full height, the spectator returns to the usual seated position.

a. Lagrangian
b. Thermodynamic limit
c. Pauli exclusion principle
d. Wave

12. The _____ is an important second-order linear partial differential equation that describes the propagation of a variety of waves, such as sound waves, light waves and water waves. It arises in fields such as acoustics, electromagnetics, and fluid dynamics. Historically, the problem of a vibrating string such as that of a musical instrument was studied by Jean le Rond d'Alembert, Leonhard Euler, Daniel Bernoulli, and Joseph-Louis Lagrange.

a. Lagrangian
b. Random walk
c. Wave equation
d. Cauchy momentum equation

13. In mathematics, particularly linear algebra and numerical analysis, the _____ is a method for orthogonalizing a set of vectors in an inner product space, most commonly the Euclidean space R^n. The _____ takes a finite, linearly independent set S = {v_1, ââ,¬¦, v_n} and generates an orthogonal set S' = {u_1, ââ,¬¦, u_n} that spans the same subspace as S.

The method is named for J>ørgen Pedersen Gram and Erhard Schmidt but it appeared earlier in the work of Laplace and Cauchy.

a. Dot product
b. Linear algebra
c. Gram-Schmidt process
d. Homogeneous coordinates

14. In statistics, _____ has two related meanings:

- the arithmetic _____.
- the expected value of a random variable, which is also called the population _____.

It is sometimes stated that the '_____' _____s average. This is incorrect if '_____' is taken in the specific sense of 'arithmetic _____' as there are different types of averages: the _____, median, and mode. For instance, average house prices almost always use the median value for the average.

For a real-valued random variable X, the _____ is the expectation of X.

a. Probability
b. Mean
c. Statistical population
d. Proportional hazards model

Chapter 12. Numerical Methods for Partial-Differential Equations

15. In calculus, the _____ states, roughly, that given a section of a smooth curve, there is at least one point on that section at which the derivative of the curve is equal to the 'average' derivative of the section. It is used to prove theorems that make global conclusions about a function on an interval starting from local hypotheses about derivatives at points of the interval.

This theorem can be understood concretely by applying it to motion: if a car travels one hundred miles in one hour, so that its average speed during that time was 100 miles per hour, then at some time its instantaneous speed must have been exactly 100 miles per hour.

    a. Calculus controversy
    b. Fundamental Theorem of Calculus
    c. Functional integration
    d. Mean Value Theorem

16. In mathematics, a _____ is a statement that can be proved on the basis of explicitly stated or previously agreed assumptions.

    a. Logical value
    b. Theorem
    c. Boolean function
    d. Disjunction introduction

17. In mathematics, the _____ is an approach to finding a particular solution to certain inhomogeneous ordinary differential equations and recurrence relations. It is closely related to the annihilator method, but instead of using a particular kind of differential operator in order to find the best possible form of the particular solution, a 'guess' is made as to the appropriate form, which is then tested by differentiating the resulting equation. In this sense, the _____ is less formal but more intuitive than the annihilator method.

    a. Linear differential equation
    b. Method of undetermined coefficients
    c. Differential algebraic equations
    d. Phase line

18. In cryptography, _____ is a block cipher designed in 2002 by Jorge Nakahara, Jr., Vincent Rijmen, Bart Preneel, and Joos Vandewalle. _____ is based directly on IDEA and uses the same basic operations.

_____ is actually a family of 3 variant ciphers with block sizes of 64, 96, and 128 bits.

    a. Depth
    b. Key server
    c. Mesh
    d. Duality

19. A _____ is a large fiber or metal rope, used for hauling, lifting or an assembly of two or more insulated electrical conductors, laid up together as an assembly. An optical _____ contains one or more optical fibers in a protective jacket that supports the fibers.

Ropes made of multiple strands of natural fibers such as hemp, sisal, manila, and cotton have been used for millennia for hoisting and hauling.

    a. 120-cell
    b. 1-center problem
    c. 2-3 heap
    d. Cable

20. In geometry, _____ means that two or more forms share a common axis; it is the three-dimensional linear analog of 'concentric'.

_____ cable, as a common example, has a wire conductor in the center a circumferential outer conductor and an insulating medium called the dielectric separating these two conductors. The outer conductor is usually sheathed in a protective PVC outer jacket.

a. Flatness
b. Lateral surface
c. Coaxial
d. Codimension

21. In mathematics and in the sciences, a _____ (plural: _____e, formulæ or _____s) is a concise way of expressing information symbolically (as in a mathematical or chemical _____), or a general relationship between quantities. One of many famous _____e is Albert Einstein's E = mc² (see special relativity

In mathematics, a _____ is a key to solve an equation with variables. For example, the problem of determining the volume of a sphere is one that requires a significant amount of integral calculus to solve.

a. 120-cell
b. 1-center problem
c. 2-3 heap
d. Formula

22. In model theory, a complete theory is called _____ if it does not have too many types. One goal of classification theory is to divide all complete theories into those whose models can be classified and those whose models are too complicated to classify, and to classify all models in the cases where this can be done. Roughly speaking, if a theory is not _____ then its models are too complicated and numerous to classify, while if a theory is _____ there might be some hope of classifying its models, especially if the theory is superstable or totally transcendental.

a. Transfer principle
b. Spectrum of a theory
c. Non-standard calculus
d. Stable

23. In the mathematical subfield of numerical analysis, a _____ is a spline function that has minimal support with respect to a given degree, smoothness, and domain partition. A fundamental theorem states that every spline function of a given degree, smoothness, and domain partition, can be represented as a linear combination of _____s of that same degree and smoothness, and over that same partition. The term _____ was coined by Isaac Jacob Schoenberg and is short for basis spline.

a. 1-center problem
b. B-spline
c. Non-uniform rational B-spline
d. Cubic Hermite spline

24. The _____ is an important partial differential equation which describes the distribution of heat in a given region over time. For a function u

$$\frac{\partial u}{\partial t} - k\left(\frac{\partial^2 u}{\partial x^2} + \frac{\partial^2 u}{\partial y^2} + \frac{\partial^2 u}{\partial z^2}\right) = 0$$

where k is a constant.

The _____ is of fundamental importance in diverse scientific fields.

Chapter 12. Numerical Methods for Partial-Differential Equations

a. 120-cell
c. 1-center problem
b. 2-3 heap
d. Heat Equation

25. In mathematics, a _____ is a quadric surface, with the following equation in Cartesian coordinates: $(x/_a)^2 + (y/_b)^2 = 1$.

a. Derivative algebra
c. Free
b. Discontinuity
d. Cylinder

26. In linear algebra, _____ is an efficient algorithm for solving systems of linear equations, finding the rank of a matrix, and calculating the inverse of an invertible square matrix. _____ is named after German mathematician and scientist Carl Friedrich Gauss.

Elementary row operations are used to reduce a matrix to row echelon form.

a. Cholesky decomposition
c. Conjugate gradient method
b. Gaussian elimination
d. Crout matrix decomposition

27. In applied mathematics and mechanical engineering, the _____ is a widely used, classical method for the calculation of the natural vibration frequency of a structure in the second or higher order. It is a direct variational method in which the minimum of a functional defined on a normed linear space is approximated by a linear combination of elements from that space. This method will yield solutions when an analytical form for the true solution may be intractable.

a. 120-cell
c. 1-center problem
b. 2-3 heap
d. Rayleigh-Ritz method

28. In mathematics, a _____ is a system which is not linear. Less technically, a _____ is any problem where the variabl to be solved for cannot be written as a linear sum of independent components. A nonhomogenous system, which is linear apart from the presence of a function of the independent variables, is nonlinear according to a strict definition, but such systems are usually studied alongside linear systems, because they can be transformed to a linear system as long as a particular solution is known.

a. George Dantzig
c. Metric system
b. 1-center problem
d. Nonlinear system

29. In mathematics, a _____ is an expression constructed from variables and constants, using the operations of addition, subtraction, multiplication, and constant non-negative whole number exponents. For example, $x^2 - 4x + 7$ is a _____, but $x^2 - 4/x + 7x^{3/2}$ is not, because its second term involves division by the variable x and also because its third term contains an exponent that is not a whole number.

_____s are one of the most important concepts in algebra and throughout mathematics and science.

a. Semifield
c. Group extension
b. Coimage
d. Polynomial

30. In linear algebra, a _____ is a set of vectors that, in a linear combination, can represent every vector in a given vector space or free module, and such that no element of the set can be represented as a linear combination of the others. In other words, a _____ is a linearly independent spanning set. This picture illustrates the standard _____ in R^2.

Chapter 12. Numerical Methods for Partial-Differential Equations

a. Conchoid
c. Basis
b. Chiral
d. Dot plot

31. In mathematics, particularly numerical analysis, a _____ is an element of the basis for a function space. The term is a degeneration of the term basis vector for a more general vector space; that is, each function in the function space can be represented as a linear combination of the _____s.

The collection of quadratic polynomials with real coefficients has $\{1, t, t^2\}$ as a basis.

a. Bernstein polynomial
c. Meshfree methods
b. Constructions of low-discrepancy sequences
d. Basis function

32. The mathematical concept of a _____ expresses the intuitive idea of deterministic dependence between two quantities, one of which is viewed as primary and the other as secondary. A _____ then is a way to associate a unique output for each input of a specified type, for example, a real number or an element of a given set.

a. Function
c. Grill
b. Coherent
d. Going up

33. In mathematics, an _____ or member of a set is any one of the distinct objects that make up that set.

Writing A = {1,2,3,4}, means that the _____s of the set A are the numbers 1, 2, 3 and 4. Groups of _____s of A, for example {1,2}, are subsets of A.

a. Order
c. Universal code
b. Ideal
d. Element

34. _____ is a finite element analysis (FEA) program that was originally developed for NASA in the late 1960s under United States government funding for the Aerospace industry. The MacNeal-Schwendler Corporation (MSC) was one of the principal and original developers of the public domain _____ code. _____ source code is integrated in a number of different software packages, which are distributed by a range of companies.

a. Femap
c. NASTRAN
b. LS-DYNA
d. SAMCEF

ANSWER KEY

Chapter 1
1. d   2. d   3. b   4. d   5. d   6. d   7. a   8. d   9. d   10. b
11. d   12. c   13. d   14. a   15. d   16. b   17. d   18. d   19. a   20. d
21. b   22. d   23. d   24. a   25. d   26. d   27. b   28. c   29. b   30. a
31. d   32. d   33. b   34. b   35. a   36. d   37. b   38. c   39. b   40. d
41. d   42. c   43. d   44. d   45. d   46. d

Chapter 2
1. a   2. b   3. d   4. b   5. a   6. d   7. d   8. d   9. c   10. b
11. c   12. a   13. a   14. c   15. d   16. d   17. d   18. a   19. a   20. d
21. c   22. d   23. a   24. d   25. d   26. d   27. d

Chapter 3
1. a   2. b   3. a   4. a   5. d   6. d   7. c   8. d   9. d   10. d
11. b   12. b   13. a   14. b   15. a   16. d   17. b   18. c   19. c   20. a
21. c   22. a   23. c   24. c   25. d   26. b   27. d   28. a   29. a   30. d
31. c   32. d

Chapter 4
1. c   2. d   3. b   4. a   5. a   6. a   7. d   8. d   9. d   10. d
11. a   12. d   13. c   14. b   15. a   16. d   17. d   18. c   19. d   20. d
21. d   22. c   23. d   24. d   25. a   26. d   27. a   28. a   29. b   30. c
31. a   32. d   33. d   34. a   35. a   36. d   37. c

Chapter 5
1. b   2. a   3. d   4. a   5. a   6. a   7. b   8. d   9. d   10. d
11. d   12. d   13. a   14. d   15. d   16. b   17. a   18. c   19. d   20. d
21. c   22. c   23. d   24. d   25. d   26. a   27. c   28. d   29. d   30. b
31. c   32. d   33. d   34. d   35. d

Chapter 6
1. d   2. a   3. a   4. b   5. a   6. c   7. d   8. d   9. d   10. d
11. b   12. d   13. d   14. d   15. d   16. a   17. d   18. d   19. d   20. b
21. d   22. b   23. d   24. d   25. c   26. c   27. a   28. d   29. a   30. b
31. d   32. a   33. b   34. d   35. d   36. b   37. d   38. d   39. d   40. c
41. b   42. c   43. d   44. b   45. d   46. b   47. a   48. c   49. a   50. d
51. d   52. b

Chapter 7
1. d   2. d   3. d   4. b   5. d   6. b   7. d   8. b   9. d   10. d
11. d   12. c   13. b   14. c   15. b   16. d   17. d   18. d   19. a   20. d
21. d   22. d   23. c   24. a   25. d   26. a   27. d   28. a   29. a   30. b
31. a   32. c   33. a   34. a   35. c   36. d   37. a   38. d   39. c   40. a
41. d   42. d   43. d

Chapter 8

1. a	2. d	3. d	4. d	5. d	6. d	7. d	8. c	9. d	10. d
11. d	12. a	13. b	14. c	15. c	16. b	17. c	18. a	19. d	20. b
21. d	22. d	23. c	24. a	25. c	26. d	27. c	28. a	29. c	30. c
31. d	32. a	33. d	34. d	35. d	36. d	37. d	38. a	39. b	40. d
41. d	42. d								

Chapter 9

1. b	2. d	3. d	4. c	5. b	6. d	7. d	8. d	9. d	10. d
11. a	12. d	13. d	14. b	15. d	16. a	17. d	18. d	19. d	20. a
21. b	22. a	23. d	24. b	25. b	26. d	27. d	28. d	29. a	30. d
31. d	32. d								

Chapter 10

1. d	2. c	3. b	4. d	5. d	6. b	7. a	8. b	9. b	10. c
11. d	12. d	13. d	14. d	15. b	16. d	17. d	18. a	19. a	20. b

Chapter 11

1. a	2. d	3. d	4. b	5. b	6. d	7. d	8. d	9. a	10. d
11. d	12. d	13. d	14. d	15. b	16. b	17. d	18. b	19. c	20. d
21. c	22. a	23. d	24. d	25. a					

Chapter 12

1. b	2. d	3. a	4. c	5. d	6. d	7. d	8. b	9. d	10. b
11. d	12. c	13. c	14. b	15. d	16. b	17. b	18. c	19. d	20. c
21. d	22. d	23. b	24. d	25. d	26. b	27. d	28. d	29. d	30. c
31. d	32. a	33. d	34. c